NAMES OF PERSONS

WHO TOOK THE

Oath of Allegiance to the State of Pennsylvania,

BETWEEN THE YEARS 1777 AND 1789,

WITH

A HISTORY OF THE "TEST LAWS" OF PENNSYLVANIA.

BY

THOMPSON WESTCOTT.

Southern Historical Press, Inc.
Greenville, South Carolina

This volume was reprupuced from
a personal copy located in the
Publisher's private library
Greenville, South Carolina

All rights reserved. No part of this publication may be reproduced, stored in a retieval system, Transmitted in any form, posted on to the web in any form or by any means without the prior permission of the publisher.

Please direct ALL correspondence and book orders to:
www.southernhistoricalpress.com
or
**Southern Historical Press, Inc.
PO Box 1267
Greenville, SC 29602-1267
southernhistoricalpress@gmail.com**

Originally published: Philadelphia, PA 1865
ISBN #978-1-63914-035-0
All Rights Reserved
Printed in the United States of America

HISTORY

OF THE

"TEST LAWS" OF PENNSYLVANIA.

A HISTORY

OF THE

"TEST LAWS" AND LAWS CONCERNING "OATHS OF ALLEGIANCE" IN FORCE IN PENNSYLVANIA BETWEEN JUNE 13, 1777, AND MARCH 13, 1789.

THE breaking out of the American Revolution found the British Colonies in North America under the domination of laws, customs and opinions, which exercised a strong influence upon the mass of the people, and which even had their effect upon those patriots who were most sanguine in opposition to the measures of the British government. However eager they might have been in the assertion of their independent principles, and whatsoever their sympathies in favor of reform, they had to submit in a degree to ancient habits, which, with inveterate mannerism, controlled radical aspirations. Pennsylvania, which was one of the most important of the colonies, was under the dominancy of a religious sect which had been at all times opposed to wars and fighting; its meetings had borne frequent testimony upon those subjects, and the sincerity of its members could not be doubted. Added to these conscientious convictions were their political opinions and their interests. They were generally men of substance and property, who took delight in thrift, and were never so well satisfied as when they were increasing their wealth. They could not anticipate in the agitations of war anything else but a derangement of society, a diversion of the industry of the country from settled modes, violence, destruction of property, heavy taxation, and an enormous debt. Their religion and their interests therefore rendered them friends of the royal government, and, in consequence of their unwillingness to take part with the popular party, the reins of power which they had steadily held in Pennsylvania for ninety-four years slipped from their grasp. New men arose to hold the offices of State, and the political power of the Society of Friends in the Colony and State was so thoroughly broken that from that time its members have ceased to be politicians, in the ordinary meaning of that word.

With the Quakers, there were joined on the side of the opponents of the American Revolution native and British born sympathizers with the royal cause, who, with all others of the same manner of thinking, received the party name of "Tories." These men formed a very powerful minority in Pennsylvania, which, however, in consequence of the passive principles of non-resistance entertained by the Society of Friends, gave but little trouble in comparison to what might have been done had the members of the latter been disposed to meddle in public affairs, and to have gone to the lengths which were sought to be reached by their more active and virulent Tory associates. The element of dissatisfaction was, nevertheless, strong, and occasionally very determined measures were necessary in dealing with it.

Until after the Declaration of Independence, and the institution of a new State government, the Assembly of the Province of Pennsylvania occupied somewhat of a subordinate position. There was a general distrust of its members. They were elected under the Royal Government, and their enthusiasm in the patriot cause was not extravagant. It is true that they voted permission to defend the Province, and authorized the raising of troops, but they merely sanctioned what had already been done, which they could not prevent, and the command of the soldiers was in the hands of city and county committees elected by citizens. These committees were generally composed of unflinching Whigs, and their activity, patriotism and just dealing are conspicuous in the annals of the times. They would allow of no measures hostile to the popular cause, and they kept a stiff curb upon the tongues of Tories, who were inclined to be obstreperous or violent in their attacks upon the prevailing policy. They stimulated the raising of troops, prepared the equipments and supplies, regulated measures for meeting the expenses, and generally managed the affairs of their respective neighborhoods.*

* The following humiliating recantations made in 1775 show the severity of these bodies, and the manner in which they compelled the disaffected to publicly acknowledge their errors.

PHILADELPHIA, July 14, 1775. Whereas I have some time past, frequently made use of rash and imprudent expressions, with respect to the conduct of my fellow-citizens, who are now engaged in a noble and patriotic struggle against the arbitrary measures of the British Ministry, which conduct has justly raised their resentments against me. I now confess that I have acted extremely wrong in so doing, for which I am exceedingly sorry, and humbly ask pardon, and forgiveness of the public, and I do solemnly promise that I will for the future conduct myself in such a manner, as to avoid giving any offence. And at the same time in justice to myself, must declare that I am not unfriendly to the present measures pursued by the friends of American Liberty, but do heartily approve of them, and as far as in my power will endeavor to promote them. AMOS WICKERSHAM.

PHILADELPHIA, July 17, 1775. Whereas I have spoken disrespectfully of the General Congress, as well as of these military gentlemen who have associated for the defence of the Liberties of America. I now take this opportunity of declaring that

The first troops raised were volunteers, and they bore the general title "Associators," from the fact that they had associated together for general defence. The title was an old one, and had been used to designate the volunteer citizen soldiers who had united to defend the Province before the Revolution during the British and French wars. These forces were at times considerable. The Assemblies, under Quaker influence, having refused to allow their equipment, they were authorized by the Governors of the Province, act-

my conduct proceeded from the most contracted notions of the British Constitution, and of the rights of human nature. I am sorry for my guilt, and am ashamed of my folly. I now believe all assemblies to be legal and constitutional which are framed by the united suffrages of a free people, and am convinced that no soldiers are so respectable as those who take up arms in defence of liberty. I believe that Kings are to be no longer feared or obeyed than while they execute just laws, and that a corrupted British Ministry with a venal Parliament at their heels are now attempting to reduce the American Colonies to the lowest degrees of slavery. I most sincerely wish the counsels of Congress may be always directed with wisdom, and that the arms of America may always be crowned with success, and I pray that every man in America who behaves as I have formerly done, may *not* meet with the lenity which I have experienced, but may be obliged to expiate his crimes in a more ignominious manner.

MORDECAI LEVY.

This humiliating recantation was made in the presence of a large concourse of people, as appears from the following extract from Christopher Marshall's Diary.

"17*th July*. Stayed at home till near six, took a walk to the College yard to see the Dutch butcher ask pardon of one of the companies for speaking disrespectfully of their proceedings."

The following was published about a month afterward.

WHEREAS it has been made to appear by the evidence of several of my fellow-citizens that I, John Bergum, have made use of sundry expressions derogatory to the liberties of this country. I hereby confess myself very much to blame for my behaviour, and do promise that I will for the future conduct myself as a true friend to America and assist those of the inhabitants thereof who are now struggling against arbitrary power, by every means I am capable of, and do freely and without constraint agree that this declaration be published in the newspapers of this city. As witness my hand.

JOHN BERGUM,
Inkeeper, Sign of the Bull's Head, Strawberry Alley.

Jabez Maud Fisher was brought before the people at the Coffee House in April, and compelled to acknowledge who was the author of a letter to him from Duck Creek, reflecting on the popular sentiment. Jabez was allowed to go with some reluctance, after giving the name of Robert Halliday, of Duck Creek, as writer of the letter. A day or two afterward, Thomas Loosley, shoemaker, at the same place was "exalted as a spectacle," and compelled to beg pardon for having villified Congress.

ing under instructions from the Penn family, which, after the decease of its illustrious member, William Penn, had turned aside from Quakerdom and returned to the Church of England. During the greater portion of the term of the Revolutionary War, the Associators, with the local committees, and the committees which administered the government of the State had great influence in county affairs, and shaped them very much to their own liking.*

* The following are some notable evidences of the control which was maintained over the disaffected.

In Committee, March 1, 1776.

Herr Juncken of this City having voluntarily sent to this Committee the following letter which is voted a proper acknowledgement of his own, Ordered that the same be published in all the papers English and German in and near this city.

T. MATLACK, *Sec. Pro Tem.*

GENTLEMEN:—Whereas I have been charged before you of being inimical to the noble struggle for liberty in general as well as to the Association in particular: and whereas there may have words dropped in conversation which may be construed as tending to discourage those which otherwise would have associated, the which was never my intention to do. And whereas I value liberty as dear as life, and am sensible that I shall reap a proportionable benefit in the success of this our noble struggle for the same, my interest and that of the public being inseparably connected. And whereas I am sorry for any unguarded word which may have dropped from my mouth and which may convey even the most distant sense of being inimicably disposed to this our noble struggle, being also deeply concerned for the displeasure of the public in general as well as my respected fellow-citizens in particular, for whom I have nothing but good will at heart and with whom I wish to live in peace, harmony and friendship: therefore to appease their minds, and to convince the public in general that this my declaration is sincere, and that I am not insensible of the duty of my country, I do hereby of my own free will and accord and without any persuasion, threat or compulsion whatever ask their pardon for any offence by me to them or any of them given. My future conduct will and shall prove that I am equally with them engaged in the same good cause, and that I am determined (as I have always been) to stand or fall with them in this our noble struggle for LIBERTY.

To the Gentlemen of the Committee of Inspection.

To the Committee of Inspection and Observation of the City and Liberties of Philadelphia.

PHILADA., *April* 2, 1776.

GENTLEMEN:—I am very sorry that I have exceeded the limits prescribed by you for the price of coffee. Had I apprehended that advancing one penny per pound more than you had fixed, would have been considered as injurious to the public welfare I should not have demanded it. As I have thereby given offence, I take this method of acknowledging my error and to declare that for the future I will avoid every occasion of uneasiness to my fellow-citizens. Should you think it necessary to

The Society of Friends maintained its hostility to the principles of the Revolution by the promulgation of opinions in which its members, by a non-resistant policy, were quite as powerful as by open opposition. It was a long time before the leading men of this sect could perceive that power had departed from the crown forever. As late as January 20, 1776, the yearly meeting of the Society of Friends assembled at Philadelphia, issued "the ancient testimony and principles of the people, called Quakers, renewed with respect to the King's government, and touching the commotions now prevailing in these and other parts of America, addressed to the people in general." In that address, among other sentiments unfriendly to the cause of American liberty appeared the following language.

"The benefits, advantages and favours we have experienced by our dependence upon the connection with the King's Government, under which we have enjoyed this happy state, appear to demand from us the greatest circumspection, care, and constant endeavours to guard against every attempt to alter or

publish what is past on this subject, I request you will at the same time let this acknowledgment accompany it, and you will thereby oblige
Gentlemen, your most humble servant,
WILLIAM SITGREAVES.

To the Committee of Inspection and Observation of the City and Liberties of Philadelphia.

GENTLEMEN:—The mistake which I have committed in having bought and sold two barrels of coffee, at a price higher than limited by you, gives me extreme pain. Had I adverted to the fatal consequences of such conduct, the regard I have for the public welfare and the interest I have taken in the present struggle for liberty, would have wholly prevented my having *any share* in so destructive a measure. I now voluntarily offer to the public through the Committee my sincere acknowledgment for this error, and declare the utmost readiness to acquiesce in any measure that may assure the public of my exact conformity in future, to such regulations as this Committee may judge to be for the public benefit—being fully satisfied of their unbiassed attention to the public good. If this Committee should judge it necessary, to publish my case to the world, I shall hold myself extremely obliged if they shall judge it proper, to suffer this declaration and acknowledgment to appear at the same time and order it accordingly. PETER OZEAS.

PHILADELPHIA, *April* 2, [1776.]

subvert that dependence and connection. * * * * * May we therefore firmly unite in the abhorrence of all such writings and measures, as evidence a desire and a design to break off the happy connection we have hitherto enjoyed with the Kingdom of Great Britain, and our just and necessary subordination to the King and those lawfully placed in authority under him."*

* The sentiments of this testimony were more thoroughly illustrated in the following composition, which was not published until Philadelphia was occupied by the British army.

AMERICAN LIBERTY EXPLAINED.

AS UNDERSTOOD IN PHILADELPHIA IN THE SPRING OF THE YEAR 1776.

By Philadelphus Tranquillius.

What is Congressional liberty?
To violate the public tranquillity.
What is Conventional liberty?
To overturn the Constitution.
What is Committorial liberty?
To destroy the laws.
What is Presbyterian liberty?
To persecute the Quakers and all others in their power who differ in opinion from the Presbyterians.
. What is the general liberty of the Colonies, which are now under the dominion of Congress?
Extreme anarchy, or the worst of tyranny.

> BEHOLD, O land of boasted liberty,
> The state to which thy sons have hurried thee.
> Thy Patriots banished and thy Charters torn,
> Thy cities languish, and thy sages mourn.
> By thy own hands this misery is brought,
> By thy own hands are all these evils wrought.
> By thy own hands thy sons untimely slain,
> Thy freedom lost, shalt thou lament in vain,
> Nor less *Sylvania*, these thy acts declare,
> Who can remember thee without a tear.
> Policy, too wise, for savage minds to choose,
> Freedom, too great, for wicked hands to use.
> A State more happy never known before,
> By thy own parracide are now no more.*
> Remotest nations shall astonished hear,
> What *hellish* rage could operate so far.
> Succeeding ages shall with wonder read,
> And late posterity shall curse the deed.

---

* The unhappy catastrophe in the State of Pennsylvania appears to have been plainly predicted by the founder of the Province, W. Penn, who, in a letter to one

The most active friends of liberty were the Associators. They were dissatisfied with the proceedings of the Assembly. On the 14th of June, 1776, they addressed a strong remonstrance to that body. They averred that it was notorious that many members of the House were opposed to military defence. There were representatives among them, who, since the beginning of the opposition to Great Britain, had refused to concur in proper measures for the safety of the people. The Assembly had *never prepared any obligation* to bind its own members to the popular cause. They still put at the head of their proceedings, "John Penn, Governor," and seemed to sympathize with the old system. They had shown so little interest in the resistance to ministerial tyranny, as to put a fine of 3s. 6d. per day on non-Associators for every day of neglect to attend muster, and that, too, in so lax a manner that it was doubtful whether the penalties could ever be collected. The members had been elected by those who acknowledged King George. They were not to be trusted with the appointment of Generals to command the Associators, lest they would give them such "as would enable a certain party to make up with the enemy at the expense of our lives and liberties." The Assembly received this chiding in meekness; it was powerless to resist insult, and what in calmer times would have been high breach of privilege, was submitted to. The Associators of Philadelphia carried out their measures of defiance by issuing circulars to all the

of his friends, respecting it, has the following remarkable expressions, viz: "to conclude it is now in Friends hands. Thro' my travail, faith and patience it came. If Friends here keep to God, and in the justice, mercy, equity and fear of the Lord, their enemies will be their footstools. If not their heirs and my heirs too, will loose all, and desolation will follow "—*Penn's Life and Works.*

Associators in the State, inviting a meeting of delegates at Lancaster on the 4th of July, to choose two Brigadier-generals. Fifty-three battalions participated in that Convention, and they elected Daniel Roberdeau and James Ewing, Generals.

Congress had, in May, [1776], upon motion of John Adams, recommended that where no "State Government existed sufficient for the exigencies of affairs, that such form of government should be adopted, as in the opinion of the majority of the people would best conduce to the happiness and safety of their constituents in particular, and America in general." The preamble to this resolution declared that it was "irreconcilable to reason and good conscience that the American people should take the *oaths* for the support of government under the crown of Great Britain," and that it was "necessary that every kind of authority under the crown should be suppressed." A struggle at once commenced as to the manner in which the new government should be authorized in Pennsylvania. The Tories and Moderates argued that the Assembly was a sufficient government, and that no other was needed. The Whigs insisted that a conference should be held for the adoption of a State Constitution. The Committee of Inspection of the City and Liberties boldly attacked the authority of "the Justices of his Majesty, George III's Court of Quarter Sessions, and Common Pleas," stating the resolution of Congress against oaths of allegiance and in favor of the suppression of royal governments, "and asking the Justices to surcease the exercise of any authority in the present Courts, and until a new government is framed." The obligation of a Grand Juror they said "is incompatible with the opposition to the King and to the resolves of Congress."

The Associators of Philadelphia, in five battalions, resolved to sustain the measures for the suppression of the old government. The Committee of Inspection sent out messengers into the counties to stir up their committees on this subject, and the result was that a conference of these committees met at Carpenter's Hall on the 18th of June, and elected Thomas McKean, President, Joseph Hart, Vice President, and Jonathan B. Smith and Samuel Cadwalader Morris, Secretaries. It was voted that it was necessary to call a Provincial Convention to form a new government, on the authority of the people only. It was also resolved, that no person elected to serve as a member of the Convention should take his seat or give his vote until he should have made and subscribed the following declaration:

I, —— ——, do profess faith in God the Father and in Jesus Christ his Eternal Son, the true God, and in the Holy Spirit one God blessed evermore, and do acknowledge the sacred Scriptures of the Old and New Testament to be given by Divine inspiration.

This religious test was not well received in some quarters, and gave rise to considerable dissatisfaction.

The Convention met on the 15th of July, and during its session it not only discussed and perfected the measures necessary in the adoption of a constitution, but assumed the supreme authority in the State, and legislated upon matters foreign to the object for which it was convened. Benjamin Franklin was the President, George Ross, Vice President, John Morris, Secretary, and Jacob Garrigues, Assistant Secretary. Among other matters this body appointed a Council of Safety, to carry on the Executive duties of the Government, approved of the Declaration of Independence, and appointed Justices of the Peace, who were required before assuming their functions to each take an oath of renunciation of the authority of George III., and one of allegiance to the State of Pennsylvania. The old Assembly, which had adjourned on the 14th of June, to meet on the 14th of August, could not obtain a quorum, and adjourned again to the 23d of September. It then interposed a feeble remonstrance against the invasion of its prerogatives by the Convention, but it was a dying protest. The Declaration of Independence had given the old State Government a mortal blow, and it soon expired without a sigh—thus ending forever the proprietary and royal authority in Pennsylvania.

The Convention adopted a Constitution on the 28th of September, which immediately went into operation. It provided for a single Assembly, without a Senate, and the Executive power was reposed in the Supreme Executive Council of twelve members. Members of the Assembly before taking their seats were obliged to take an oath or affirmation to support the Constitution, and to act faithfully, and to subscribe a declaration of a belief in one God the Creator and Governor of the Universe, the rewarder of the good and the punisher of the wicked, and that the Scriptures of the Old and New Testament were given by divine inspiration.

An objection to the test prescribed for members of the Convention was, that it compelled a recognition of the Christian religion; an objection to this test for members of the Assembly was that it did not. The persons who were dissatisfied with the new obligation, objected, that "a belief in Jesus Christ was not required, which would admit professed Deists, Jews, Mohammedans, and other enemies of Christ into the Assembly, and whether there is not in fact a firmer establishment for anti-Christ, and all damnable errors, than the Quebec bill, for Popery, let the world judge."

The Quakers still remained stubborn, notwithstanding the Declaration of Independence and the accession of the new State Government. On the 20th of December, they issued a new "testimony of Friends in Pennsylvania and New Jersey," in which, among other things, they urged a patient spirit, "that we may with Christian firmness and fortitude withstand and refuse to submit to the arbitrary injunctions and ordinances of men who assume to themselves the power of compelling others, either in person or by other assistance to aid in carrying on war, and of prescribing modes of religions, and laws concerning our religious principles, by *imposing tests not warranted by the precepts of Christ*, or the laws of the happy Constitution under which we and others *long enjoyed* tranquillity and peace."

Political disputes were renewed in the succeeding year, [1777], but not with the virulence which was manifested immediately after the adoption of the Constitution. The members of the State Navy Board, appointed by the Supreme Executive Council in March, refused to take the oath of allegiance to the State, but declared themselves willing to take the oath of allegiance to the United States. The Council was undecided what to do, and no action being taken the recusants remained in their offices.

It was now time to make some better arrangements for defence and providing for the service of troops than had yet been authorized in the State. The Association had been tried, and was found not to be reliable. The men being volunteers, and not being even bound by law of the State, followed their own desires in serving or withdrawing from duty when called upon. The Pennsylvania Associators, when sent to Amboy in the summer of 1776, had been tried, and, although they were not in action, their strength was continually depressed by withdrawals of the men, who went home. At the battle of Princeton, the only Association Company which distinguished itself was the City Troop, which, notwithstanding its strength at home, furnished only twenty-six officers and men, at a time of great peril. The Country Associators after this battle deserted in full bodies, leaving only their officers, and in one case spoken of by General Putnam, "only a lieutenant and a lame man." A more stringent system was needed, and this necessity was provided for by the Legislature in a general militia law, which was passed June 13, 1777. This act made full provisions for the enrolment of persons fit for military duty, in districts, each containing enough citizens to form a battalion of not less than 640 men, nor more than 680 men. They were to be commanded by enrolling officers, who were to be sub-lieutenants for the districts, and by lieutenants for each county. There were many details in the law which need not be specified here. But, in addition to the military regulations laid down in this act, there were other provisions of importance to every citizen. These related to the establishment of a test and oath of allegiance, being the first instance in which a test oath had been demanded except of public officers. The measure was considered necessary, to restrain the insolence of the Tories, and the Assembly combined the objects of defending the State against foreign and domestic enemies in the same law. The preamble which introduced the sections concerning the oath of allegiance was in the following words:

Whereas, from sordid or mercenary motives, or other causes inconsistent with the happiness of a free and independent people, sundry persons have, or may yet be induced to withhold their service and allegiance from the Commonwealth of Pennsylvania as a free and independent State, as declared by Congress:

And whereas, sundry other persons in their several capacities, have at the risk of their lives and fortunes, or both, rendered great and eminent services in defence and support of the said independence, and may yet continue to do the same, and as both these sorts of persons remain at this time mixed, and in some measure undistinguished from each other, and the disaffected deriving undeserved service from the faithful and well affected; *and whereas*, allegiance and protection are reciprocal, and those who will not bear the former are not nor ought to be entitled to the benefits of the latter.

Therefore it is enacted, etc., that all white male inhabitants of the State, except of the counties of Bedford and Westmoreland, above the age of eighteen years, shall before the 1st day of the ensuing July and in the excepted counties before the 1st day of August, take and subscribe before some Justice of the Peace an *oath* in the following form:

I, —— ——, do swear or affirm, that I renounce and refuse all allegiance to George the Third, King of Great Britain, his heirs and successors: and that I will be faithful and bear true allegiance to the Commonwealth of Pennsylvania, as a free and independent State, and that I will not at any time do or cause to be done any matter or thing that will be prejudicial or injurious to the freedom and independence thereof, as declared by Congress; and also, that I will discover and make known to some one Justice of the Peace of said State all treasons or traitorous conspiracies which I now know or hereafter shall know to be formed against this or any of the United States of America.

This law which compelled those who took the oath of allegiance to forswear allegiance to the King of Great Britain, and to swear fidelity to Pennsylvania and the United States, was rendered more unpalatable to many persons by the clause compelling the citizen to reveal treasons or conspiracies of which he might have had a present knowledge, or of which he should know thereafter. It compelled him to be faithful himself, and to be an informer against others who were disloyal. It was therefore highly objectionable to many worthy people, who would have been willing to qualify themselves as to what had past, but were unwilling to bind themselves by oath to pursue any policy in the future which might compel them to either denounce some dear friend or struggle in conscience against the self-accusation that they had committed perjury. It was a very severe law, and the Legislature by additional sections added to its stringency. Whoever neglected or refused to take the oath were declared to be incapable of holding office, of serving on juries, of suing for debts, of electing or being elected, of buying, selling or transferring real estate, and they were liable to be disarmed by the lieutenant of the county. Without possession of certificates that they had taken the oath they were liable to be arrested as spies, if they traveled out of the city or county of their residence. A fine of £50 and a whipping was also menaced against every one who should forge a certificate that the oath had been taken by any person.

It was under this act that the oath was taken by the persons whose names occur in the body of this book. The record was lately discovered, and it is a valuable curiosity. Some of the names will be recognized as historical, while in other cases they will be of interest to some descendant who is well versed in the genealogy of his family.

After the passage of this act, the true Whigs flocked to the offices of the magistrates and took the oath, but the disaffected held out and still uttered their complaints against public measures. A committee of the meeting of Friends for the Northern District complained that leaden weights used for hanging windows were taken from them, and blankets were seized for the use of the soldiers. Their windows were broken, "because they would not join with the present rulers in pretended acts of devotion and conforming to their ordinances, make a show of that sort by shutting up our houses and shops professedly to observe a day of humiliation and to crave a blessing on their public proceedings, but evidently tending to spread the spirit of strife and untruth." Abuses also and destruction took place "when Friends could not illuminate their houses, and conform to such vain practices and outward marks of rejoicing to commemorate the time of these people withdrawing themselves from all subjection to the English Government and to our excellent constitution under which we long enjoyed peace and prosperity."

The continued obstinacy of the Quakers, and of the Tories generally, was borne with patience until near the time when the events of the military campaign were threatening Philadelphia. Measures were then taken to make examples of some of the more prominent men. Congress, early in September, 1777, upon some information, which, in the cool examination of a later day will not be found to have justified the measure, ordered the arrest of eleven of the principal members of the Society of Friends in Philadelphia, viz:

Joshua Fisher, Abel James, James Pemberton, Henry Drinker, Israel Pemberton, John Pemberton, John James, Samuel Pleasants, Thomas Wharton, Senr., Thomas Fisher, (son of Joshua,) and Samuel Fisher, (son of Joshua,) with all papers of a political nature in their possession, and the records and papers of the Meetings for Sufferings of the people, called Quakers. The Supreme Executive Council of the State added to the list the names of prominent Tories, some of whom were not Quakers, viz: Miers Fisher, lawyer, (son of Joshua,) Elijah Brown, Hugh Roberts, George Roberts, Joseph Fox, (formerly Barrack Master of the Province,) John Hunt, lawyer, (the father of Leigh Hunt,) Samuel Emlen, Jr., Adam Kuhn, M.D., Phineas Bond, Rev. William Smith, D.D., (Provost of the College,) Rev. Thomas Coombe, Rector of Christ Church, Samuel Shoemaker, Charles Jervis, William Drewett Smith, Charles Eddy, Thomas Pike, (dancing-master,) Owen Jones, Jr., Jeremiah Warder, William Lennot, David Lennox, Edward Pennington, Caleb Emlen, William Smith, (broker,) Samuel Murdock, Alexander Stedman, Charles Stedman, Jr., Thomas Asheton, (merchant,) William Imlay, Thomas Gilpin, Samuel Jackson, Thomas Afflick, and John Pemberton. Of these forty-two gentlemen, two, John James and Samuel Jackson, were not found. One of them, Caleb Emlen, took the oath of allegiance to the State, and was released. Dr. Adam Kuhn produced evidence that he had taken the oath of allegiance to the United States on the 2d of June. A few of these persons were ordered to be arrested at once, but the majority were given the privilege of confining themselves to their dwelling-houses, if they would refrain from doing anything injurious to the United States, and from giving intelligence to the commander of the British forces. Several of them would not comply with this request, and twenty-nine of the number were therefore arrested and confined in the Mason's Lodge, in Lodge Alley, west of Second street. After they had been there two days, they in the meanwhile being assiduous in their petitions for a hearing, which they demanded as a right, they were proffered their liberty upon taking the following oath:

I, —— ——, do swear (or affirm) that I will be faithful and bear due allegiance to the Commonwealth of Pennsylvania as an independent State.

This privilege was not generally accepted. William Imlay was released upon his parole to go to New York. Rev. Thomas Coombe was permitted to go to Virginia and thence to St. Eustatia, but twenty-one of the prisoners were sent to Virginia, where they remained under banishment for more than seven months.

The proceedings against these Tories were hurried, in consequence of the approach of the British army to Philadelphia, and during the subsequent occupation of the city there was little done by the State authorities in reference to the disloyal. It was a period of excitement and peril, and to a certain degree the functions of civil government were suspended.

After the occupation of Philadelphia the Assembly met in Lancaster. In January, 1778, an act was passed suspending the powers of the Trustees of the College and Academy at Philadelphia for a limited time, by which all the franchises of the charter were taken away. In March, an act was passed "for the attainder of divers traitors if they render not themselves by a certain day, and for vesting their estates in the Commonwealth and for ascertaining and satisfying the lawful debts and claims thereon." By this act Joseph Galloway and Andrew Allen, late members of Congress, John Allen, late member of the Committee of Inspection and Observation, William Allen the younger, late a Captain and Lieutenant-colonel of a regiment of foot in the service of the United States of America, James Rankin, of York county, Jacob Duché the younger, late Chaplain of Congress, Gilbert Hicks, of Bucks county, Samuel Shoemaker, late Alderman of Philadelphia, John Potts, of Philadelphia county, Nathaniel Vernon, late Sheriff of Chester, Christian Fouts, late Lieutenant-colonel, Lancaster, Reynold Keen, of Berks, John Biddle, of Berks, late Excise Collector of said county and Deputy Quartermaster of the United States Army, who had adhered to the King of Great Britain, were required to render themselves on or before the 20th of April to the Justices of the Supreme Court, or to any Justice of the Peace, to abide their trials for high treason. All other persons who had aided or adhered to the enemy, and who did not surrender on or before the same time were declared to be liable to attainder. The act gave to the Supreme Executive Council authority to confiscate the estates of traitors, to compel persons who were indebted to them to pay the amounts due into the treasury of the Commonwealth, and to pay honest debts due by the traitors to loyal men before the forfeiture of their property.

The attainder law was followed on the 1st of April by an act "for the better security of Government, which extended until June 1, the time for taking the oaths of allegiance to the State by all who had not subscribed that declaration." This statute specified that "all Trustees, Provosts, Rectors,

Professors, masters and tutors of any college or academy, and all schoolmasters and ushers, merchants and traders, and every person who shall act as sergeant at law, barrister, advocate, attorney, solicitor, proctor, clerk, or notary, apothecary or druggist, and every person practicing Physic or Surgery, for fee or reward," should not be allowed to act in those capacities unless they took the oath of allegiance. Any one who acted without taking such oath, was liable to a fine of £500. Justices of the Peace were authorized to summon persons who had neglected to take the oath and fine them £10, or commit them to prison for three months. Every person who would not take the oath was liable to have all firearms in his possession seized and confiscated. Persons who went into Philadelphia while it was in possession of the British without license from the Supreme Executive Council, were liable to be fined £50 each, with imprisonment, at the discretion of the Court. Persons who held office under the late Provincial Government, who did not renounce the same before the 1st of June, forfeited all their lands and tenements.

On the 25th of February, Abraham Gibbons, William Jackson, Jr., Jacob Lindley, Warner Mifflin, Joseph Husband and James Jackson, members of the Society of Friends, asked leave to lay before the Assembly then sitting at Lancaster, their sufferings under various acts of Assembly. They were ordered to be admitted to the bar of the House, but before they were allowed to speak, answers were required from them to the following questions:

1st. Whether do you acknowledge the present Assembly as the representatives of the people of the State, chosen for the purposes of legislation?

2d. Whether the people are not bound in obedience to the laws made by the Assembly agreeably to the Constitution?

The deputation, surprised at these questions, declared that they had not come prepared to answer them, and asked leave to withdraw.

The next day they made the following reply:

1st. We do believe the present Assembly to be the representatives of *a* body of the people of Pennsylvania, chosen for the purposes of legislation.

2d. We believe it to be our duty to obey the principles of grace and truth in our hearts, which is the fulfilment of all laws established in justice and righteousness. Where any decrees are made not having their foundation therein they operate against the virtuous and give liberty to the licentious, and unavoidably bring on general calamity. Although we think ourselves in duty bound to a testimony against all unrighteousness, yet it hath ever been our principle and practice, actively or passively, to submit to whatever power in the course of Providence we may live under.

The House resolved that the answers were "evasive and unsatisfactory," but it was agreed that the Quakers might petition in writing. They did so three days afterward, and asked that such of their members as were exiled to Virginia in 1777 might be released. At the same time they declared that the law requiring citizens of the State to give assurances of their allegiance to the same "infringed upon the liberty of conscience."

The persons who had been sent to Virginia were considered as prisoners of the United States and not of Pennsylvania, although the Government of the latter arrested them and sent them away. In January, the Supreme Executive Council had called the attention of Congress to their condition, and recommended their release. In March, Congress passed a resolution that they be delivered to the State. In April, the Supreme Executive Council ordered that they should be brought to Pennsylvania and set at liberty. Fifteen of them were brought back and were discharged. On the 30th of April, Thomas Gilpin and John Hunt died in exile.

On the 9th of September, [1778,] a supplement to the act "for the better security of Government" was passed, which extended the privilege of taking the oath of allegiance to persons who had been prisoners with the enemy at the time of the original passage of the law, and also to soldiers and sailors who had been in the service of the State, allowing them three months after that date or after they should come into the State. In December, a further supplement was passed, which gave to any one a right to take the oath of allegiance at any time. James Young, Plunket Fleeson, George Ord and Isaac Howell, were appointed Commissioners for the City of Philadelphia to receive the affidavits under the law, and John Moor, Jonathan B. Smith, David Knox, Seth Quee and John Richards were appointed the same officers for the county. In consequence of the passage of this act, the Supreme Executive Council issued a proclamation pardoning all persons who were confined in prison, "*convicted of pertinaciously refusing to take the several oaths or affirmations of allegiance to the State.*"

The evacuation of Philadelphia by the British, the re-occupation by the American army and the exciting events which followed, were intensified by bitter threats against the Tories, which kept that class quiet as long as the storm raged. The

Quakers, however, went on in their accustomed habits, and, notwithstanding the apparent changes in the aspect of the contest with Great Britain, refused to take notice of them. At one of their religious meetings, held 4th of 11th month, 1779, in the testimony which was signed by Isaac Zane, Clerk, they complained of injurious laws, oppressive in their nature and manner of execution, and affecting them in their liberties and privileges. They particularly mentioned a further supplement to the test laws passed in the previous session. They said, after reference to their tenets, "by the same divine principles, we are restrained from complying with injunctions and requisitions made on us of *tests*, and declarations of fidelity to either party who are engaged in actual war, lest we contradict by our conduct the profession of our faith."

A memorial setting forth these views and complaining of various personal hardships endured by the members of the Society of Friends was presented to the Assembly at the next session [1780]. It was referred to a committee, who, before making a report, addressed the following queries to members of the Society:

First. Do you acknowledge the Supreme Legislative power of the State rightfully vested in the present House of Representatives met in Assembly?

Secondly. Do you acknowledge the Supreme Executive Power of the State to be lawfully and rightfully vested in the present President and Council?

Thirdly. Do you acknowledge and agree that the same obedience and respect is due to these bodies, respectively, that you formerly paid and acknowledged to the Governor and Assembly, respectively, while Pennsylvania was dependant upon Great Britain?

Fourthly. Are you willing and do you agree to render

them the same respect and obedience you rendered the Governor and Assembly of Pennsylvania before the present war between Great Britain and America?

Fifthly. Do you consider yourselves as now living under the laws of this State, with regard to your personal liberty and property?

Sixthly. Do you admit it to be the right of the Governed to resist the Governors, where the powers of the Government are used to the oppression and destruction of the Governed?

Seventhly. Do you or do you not deem the laws passed by the King and Parliament of Great Britain for taxing this country, prohibiting its trade, sending its inhabitants to Great Britain for trial, oppressive and destructive to the people of America?

If you suppose the Continental money to be issued for the purposes of war, and therefore decline paying taxes for sinking it, or otherwise supporting its credit, you are desired to explain how you discriminate between the application of it to civil government or military purposes. And, also, why you distinguish this species of money from the emissions of paper money heretofore made by the then Province, in which civil and military purposes are blended precisely in the same manner.

And as you are specially associated together, though not incorporated in law, and issue public letters and recommendations and promulgate opinions, not only on religious but on political subjects, or at least uniting them together, you are requested to communicate the letters and testimonies which have been published from time to time for seven years past, and signed by the clerks of your General and Quarterly Meetings in this city, to be sent to other meetings, or to persons of your Society.

The reply of the Committee of Quakers, signed Isaac Zane, Jr., was not responsive to these queries in a direct way. It was suggested that "a weighty and impartial attention" to the memorial first submitted by them would show the equity and justice of their cause. After a reference to the objects for which their religious meetings were instituted, it was declared that the queries proposed to them in a religious capacity were "improper, and a mode of redressing grievances new and unprecedented, and such an inquisition on a religious society" as had never been known or heard of in America. General declarations of the ideas of the Society upon the duty of government, to promote virtue, and protect the innocent from oppression followed. The principles of the Society against war were referred to. The duty of the Society to promote the testimony of peace was declared to be a great obligation. These requirements it was averred prevented Friends from taking part in the present contest, "or joining with any measures which tend to create or promote disturbance or commotion in the Government." The reply was no answer whatever to any of the queries submitted, and it justified the assertion of the Committee of the Assembly that the answer was "couched in language so incomprehensible" that it could be considered only "as an evasion of the questions proposed." The Committee, therefore, determined that any further consideration of the subject was improper, and nothing more was done with it.

Thus matters ran on during the whole period of the war and after the negotiation of peace. The law requiring the oath of allegiance remained upon the statute book, and no effort of the Quakers, notwithstanding their numbers and influence, was of avail to produce any change. The popular mind was inflamed against the Tories for many years after the end of the war, and some angry manifestations were made against them in Philadelphia after the ratification of peace. The preliminary treaty with Great Britain contained a provision in relation to the Loyalists, guaranteeing to them a right to go to any part of the United States, and remain there for twelve months; and another, that there should be no future confiscations or prosecutions for the part they had taken in the war. To the ultra Whigs these stipulations were very unpalatable and they determined to resist them. The militia first took up the subject. At a meeting held at the State House, May 29, 1783, of which Lieut. Col. John Shee was Chairman, the following resolutions were passed:

Resolved 1st, That it is the opinion of this meeting that such persons as have joined the enemy or have been expelled from this or any other of the United States ought not to be suffered to return or remain among us. And, as officers of the City and Liberties of Philadelphia, we are determined to use all the means in our power that they shall not.

Resolved 2dly, That to attain this salutary end, we will cheerfully join with others of the community in instructions to our representatives in the Assembly.

Resolved 3dly, That persons harboring or entertaining those enemies of their country ought to feel the highest displeasure of the citizens of this City and Liberties.

Resolved 4thly, That it is the opinion of this Company that a town meeting be called as soon as possible to take into consideration the mode of instructing representatives and such other measures as may appear necessary, and that a committee be appointed to prepare for carrying this resolve into execution.

In conformance with the latter recommendation, a general meeting of citizens was held at the State House June 14th. Col. Samuel Miles was appointed Chairman, and Lieut. Col.

John Shee, Secretary. The following resolutions were agreed upon:

1st, That we consider it as inconsistent with the interest and dignity of the good people of this State, that any person who hath voluntarily withdrawn himself from this or any of the United States of America since the 19th of April, 1775, and hath joined the armies, or aided and abetted the measures employed by the King of Great Britain against this country, or who hath been legally attainted or expelled by this or any of the United States should be suffered to return to or reside within the State of Pennsylvania.

2d, That we consider it our duty as citizens and individuals to prevent any such persons returning into the State, and we do solemnly determine and mutually pledge ourselves to each other to use all the means in our power to expel with infamy such persons who have or hereafter shall presume to come among us, and that the names of such persons be published in the newspapers of this city by the committee appointed to carry these resolves into execution.

3d, That we consider the restoration of the estates forfeited by law as incompatible with the peace, the safety, and the dignity of this Commonwealth.

4th, That the dignity and interest of this State require that funds be provided for the payment and discharge of the public debt.

A committee was appointed by this meeting, which consisted of the field officers and captains of the militia of the City and Liberties. This body met at the City Tavern, and adopted a resolution giving ten days' notice to all persons coming within the description of the resolutions of the town meeting to quit the State, or that they would "be dealt with in a proper manner." A few days afterward they had before them Captain Thomas Rawlings, who was ordered to leave the State by nine o'clock on the following morning. Captain Joseph Crathorne and Thomas Plunket received a peremptory notice to depart also within a specified time. And Thomas Faro, Lancelot Faro, James Mitchell, Lawrence Fenner and Thomas Young were also warned off. The authority of the committee to act in this manner was attacked by various writers as being contrary to the treaty with Great Britain, but the committee was too strongly backed up by public opinion to be compelled to pay any attention to those remonstrances.

On the 23d of December, [1783,] the Rabbi, Ger Seixas, of the Jewish Synagogue, in Philadelphia, Simon Nathan, the *Parnass*, or President, Asher Myers, Bernard Gratz, and Haym Salomon, the *Mohammed*, or Associates of the Council, in behalf of themselves and brethren, addressed the Council of Censors in relation to the declaration required to be taken by each member of the Assembly, which affirmed that "the Scriptures of the Old and *New* Testament were given by divine inspiration;" and, also, in relation to that part of the Constitution which declared that no other religious test should be required of any civil magistrate in the State. They represented that these provisions deprived them of the right of ever becoming representatives. They did not covet office, they said, but they thought the provision improper and an injustice to the members of a persuasion that had always been attached to the American cause, and given a support to the country, some in the Continental army, some in the militia, and some by cheerfully paying taxes and cheerfully sustaining the popular cause. This memorial appeared to have no immediate effect, but it doubtless had its influence in procuring the subsequent modification of the test clause in the Constitution.

In March, [1784,] a petition to abolish the "test laws," as the laws in relation to the oath of allegiance were popularly called, was laid on the table in the Assembly by a vote of 37 yeas to 27 nays. A resolution was then offered declaring that the happy time had come to heal the divisions among the people, and that unanimity and harmony could not exist at a time when one part of the people were deprived of certain benefits which others enjoyed, and that a committee ought to be appointed to revise the law and report one more adapted to the present times. This was lost by a vote of 5 yeas to 50 nays. On the question to postpone all further consideration of the subject of the test laws the vote was 30 to 30, and the Speaker gave his casting vote in the affirmative.

A resolution was offered to the Assembly in September, stating that a large number of young men had arrived at the age of eighteen years since the passage of the test laws, who had not taken the oaths of allegiance, and were consequently deprived of interest in and attachment to the State. It was contended in this resolution that all persons should have equal rights, and the proposition concluded with a direction that a committee should be appointed to consider the subject, and, if necessary, to report a law that persons who were under the age of eighteen at the passage of the test laws should be entitled "to the blessings of liberty and citizenship." This was followed by a petition from the Non-jurors for admission to the rights of citizenship. These petitions were referred to a committee by a vote of 31 yeas to 22 nays.

In the debate which followed, a resolution was offered "that no person who voluntarily joined the British army during the war, or who had been tried or convicted of having aided or abetted the King of Great Britain, his Generals, fleets or armies, having before been a citizen of the United States, shall be capable to elect or be elected into any office of profit or trust." This was carried by a vote of 46 yeas to 4 nays. It was then proposed that a bill should be brought in to alter the test laws so as to entitle all male white inhabitants who had not theretofore taken the oath of allegiance to take the oath according to the directions of the act of 13th of June, 1777, and be thereby entitled to be free citizens: *Provided*, that no person should be capable of holding any office until he had taken and subscribed the oath directed by the act of 5th December, 1778. On this proposition the vote was, on the 25th of September, [1784,] 29 yeas to 22 nays.

This result caused a very great excitement, not only in the Assembly but among the people, and led to a scene of violence unparalleled in the history of the State. On the 28th of September, a motion to take up the bill entitled "A further supplement to the Test Laws" was followed by a vote of 25 yeas to 25 nays. The Speaker, George Gray, gave his casting vote in the affirmative. Upon this nineteen members arose in great confusion, and left the Assembly without a quorum. There could be no formal adjournment, and the session was thus suddenly and violently closed. The seceders published an address, in which they averred that attempts were made to press the bill through, in despite of the rules and without the usual formalities. They also declared that those who refused to participate in the toils and sufferings of the contest with Great Britain should not be permitted to participate in the benefits of the late Revolution. If, through motives of timidity, avarice, or attachment to the cause of British tyranny they refused to enrol their names in the honorable list of patriots in the season of danger, they ought not to be allowed to grasp the fruits of a prosperity to which they did not contribute. If they were admitted to citizenship, "the elections might be carried in the favor of men who execrate the alliance between the United States and his most Christian Majesty, and who still cherish the hope of a reunion with Great Britain." The seceders also objected to the passage of the bill restoring the charter of the College, which they looked upon as a precursor of a law to restore the hereditary rights of the Penn family. The latter had by a temperate memorial signed by John Penn, Senr., and John Penn, Junior, and Richard Penn, by his attorney, Tench Francis, asked that the Legislature would conform to natural equity, as far as might be, and that they would not heedlessly deprive them of rights which had existed since the foundation of Pennsylvania. The friends of the amendment to the test laws, by the representation of George Gray, the Speaker of the House, published an address censuring the seceders, and declaring that the measure for the relief of the Non-jurors was necessary, in consequence of the coming of age of many persons who were unable to subscribe the test act of 1779. They said, "the good people injured by this law are not only numerous but wealthy. They have paid their full proportion of the expense of the war either directly or indirectly, and the great majority of them have been uniformly peaceable and inoffensive during every stage of the Revolution. Why, then, should we oppress them any longer? Restore them to the rights of citizenship and they will embrace and support your government." They quoted the provision of the test act, that no person who had joined the army of the British King or who had been tried and convicted of aiding or abetting the King of Great Britain should be eligible to office, and this provision they insisted was a sufficient protection against any abuse of the privileges granted by an extension of the test act. It was estimated during the controversy that by the law of 1779, nearly one-half of the inhabitants of Pennsylvania were deprived of the privileges of citizens.

At the election held in Philadelphia in October, this question entered into the canvass—the ticket for the Assembly headed by Charles Pettit in the City, and William Coats in the County, who were opposed to the Non-jurors was successful. Pettit had 1,024 votes and Thomas Fitzsimons 781. In the County, Coats had 520 votes and Samuel Ashmead 375.

The contest was renewed before the Legislature in 1785, by petitions from the Non-jurors and by movements made by the friends of the repeal. General Anthony Wayne took advantage of the presentation of petitions by the persons deprived of their rights under those laws, to introduce a resolution to revise or repeal the test laws. The resolution which he offered recited that the principal objection at the previous session to the revision of the test laws was, that such action had not been asked by the persons whom the laws operated upon. This objection the resolution declared was removed by petitions lately presented by the Non-jurors themselves. The expediency of continuing those laws was now obviated by the peace, it was contended. General Wayne's resolution therefore directed the appointment of a committee to consider the matter. On the adoption of this preamble the vote was 14 yeas to 39 nays; but, on motion to appoint a committee to take the petitions into consideration, it was resolved that the measure should be sanctioned. The committee thus appointed brought in a very bitter report against the Nonjurors. They said:

It does not appear from any of the petitions who the subscribers are, whether aliens, attainted persons, Non-jurors or disaffected to the Government, but we are in the most charitable construction led to believe that they are the men who, on the 13th day of June, 1777, were required by a positive law of the State (then at open war together with the rest of the United States of America against the King of Great Britain, for the defence of life, liberty and every thing most valuable in the world), to renounce their former allegiance to the said King, and to give assurance on oath or affirmation of their allegiance and fidelity to this Commonwealth, under the penalty of forfeiting some of the privileges of citizens, that they refused to comply with this reasonable and necessary requisition, and voluntarily submitted to the penalty. * * * * * What the motives of these men were for refusing to give this satisfaction to their countrymen they have not told us. Nor will we positively say, but are constrained to believe that they were owing either to their being professed British subjects or enemies to liberty and the rights of mankind, or cowards, that meanly skulked to screen themselves and their property in the hour of difficulty and danger from the savage cruelties of the British army, while their country was suffering under their depredations. Can such men expect to enjoy all the privileges and advantages arising from our late glorious revolution equally with those heroes, patriots and virtuous persons, who, (next to God,) procured them at every hazard of life and fortune, not only without their assistance, but against their efforts or at least their inclinations? Yes; they say they expect it, and that they have a right to free citizenship by the Constitution. These petitioners had no share in the Declaration of Independence, in the formation of our Constitution, or in establishing them by arms. They were not of the people on whose authority only the great structure was erected. It cannot be supposed that any society would, without great caution, receive persons as members whose wishes and endeavors have been to destroy it.

After further arguments the Committee reported that "the Government had an inherent and unquestionable right to exact a test of allegiance from all persons in the State," and that "it would be impolitic and dangerous to admit persons who had been inimical to the sovereignty and independence of the State, to have a common participation in the Government so soon after the war." This report was adopted by a vote of 42 yeas to 15 nays.

When the new Assembly met in November, the Non-jurors again presented petitions for the repeal of the test law. So severely did this law operate upon certain districts that the number of freemen who were entitled to all the privileges of citizenship were not sufficient to administer the local government. The *freeholders* of Byberry, in November, sent a petition to the Assembly, stating that there were only *three* freemen among all the freeholders in the township. They had not enough to fill the offices, in consequence of which assessors and collectors, etc., had been sent to them from other townships, some of whom were unknown to them and rapacious, having seized their property and distressed them much. At that time both the collectors for Byberry were residents of another township.

The new Executive Council of the State, of which Benjamin Franklin was President, on the 11th of November, recommended a revision of the test laws in accordance with the change made in the circumstances under which the State was placed by the peace. The subject was again referred to a committee by the Assembly. Being equally divided, this committee was discharged and a new one appointed, which, reporting favorably, was ordered to bring in a bill. The manner in which this committee discharged its duty was by presenting the draft of "an act securing to this Commonwealth the fidelity and allegiance of the subjects thereof and for admitting certain persons to the rights of citizenship." The bill was before the Assembly in March, 1786. It proposed to extend to persons who had not yet taken the oath of allegiance the privilege of doing so. By the terms of the obligation, it was required that the affiant should renounce fidelity to King George the Third of Great Britain, and bear true allegiance to the State of Pennsylvania. Furthermore, that he would not thereafter "do any thing injurious to freedom, that he should declare that he had not, since the independence of the United States, voluntarily joined, abetted, aided or assisted the King of Great Britain, his Generals, fleets or armies while employed against the United States." Robert Morris moved to strike out words describing this oath to be one of abjuration, but the motion was lost. He also moved to strike out the declaration that the person taking the oath had never assisted the King, his Generals, fleets or armies, but with no better success. The bill was passed nearly in the form in which it was reported on the 5th of March, by a vote of 45 yeas to 43 nays.

The terms of this act gave but little satisfaction to the Non-jurors. At the next session, in February, 1787, citizens of Chester county remonstrated to the House against that portion of the act of 1786, which required an abjuration and a declaration that the affiant had not "joined, aided or abetted the King of Great Britain, his Generals, fleets and armies." There was still a bitter feeling against the Non-jurors, but it was evident that it was breaking down under the influence of time and reflection. For the first time since the passage of the law requiring an oath of allegiance, a committee of the Legislature reported against the general policy of the Nonjuror Act, or more properly against the necessity of continuing its provisions under a condition of affairs entirely different from those which existed during the struggle of the Revolution. The Committee of the Assembly reported in favor of a repeal of the requirements of the law which were supposed to be the most burdensome. It recommended an abrogation of the oath, and the substitution of a simple declaration of allegiance to the Commonwealth.

"An act to alter the test of allegiance to this Commonwealth, required by the Act of March 4, 1786," was afterward passed. But even this liberality was unsatisfactory to the Quakers. They generally refused to make the declaration required by the law. In July, two Quakers summoned on the Grand Jury of the County of Philadelphia were found to be disqualified, in consequence of not having made the declaration or affirmation of allegiance. Chief Justice McKean, who was on the Bench, decided that it was their duty to have subscribed the declaration; that their neglect to do so having disqualified them, they were in the same condition as if they had wilfully declined to serve. He therefore fined them £6 each as defaulting jurors, and ordered them to be committed to prison until the fine was paid. Norris Jones, one of them, refused to pay, and he was committed. The conduct of McKean was warmly attacked in the newspapers as being arbitrary. Jones remained in prison some days, but was released. It was averred that he did not pay the fine.

The succeeding year passed without any strong demonstration against the law of 1787, but the progress of time had softened the hearts of men, and taught them that many fears previously entertained were groundless.

The people of the **State** were now ready for the repeal of the regulations requiring tests and declarations of allegiance, and the opposition to their abrogation had died away. A committee appointed by the Assembly advocated the repeal of the law of 1787 in strong terms. In its report, it was said:

That however proper it may have been during the late war, when, by the division of a powerful nation it became necessary for individuals to make a solemn declaration of their attachment to one or the other of the contending parties, to your committee it appears that in times of peace and of well established government, they are not only useless but highly pernicious, by disqualifying a large body of the people from exercising many necessary offices and throwing the whole burthen thereof on others, and also by alienating the affections of tender though, perhaps, mistaken minds, from a Government which by its invidious distinctions they are led to consider as hostile to their peace and happiness.

The Committee, therefore, recommended a repeal of all test

laws. In accordance a bill was passed on the 13th of March, 1789, to repeal all laws requiring any oath or affirmation of allegiance "from the inhabitants of the State." Persons disfranchised by former laws were restored to citizenship. Foreigners only were required to take an oath of allegiance upon assuming the privileges of citizens. The names of the latter were to be registered by the Recorders of Deeds.

The adoption of the new Constitution of the State of Pennsylvania, in 1790, disposed of the obnoxious religious test which yet remained in the Constitution of 1776. It also released many conscientious persons from the obligation of the oath that they would "not do or say any thing directly or indirectly that would be injurious or prejudicial to the Constitution as established by the Convention." There was thenceforth no State oath of allegiance, except where the same was administered to public officers, and to all such obligations there were added a pledge to support and defend the Constitution of the United States. The test laws of Pennsylvania had passed away with the occasion that gave rise to them, and in the progress of time the angry passions engendered by the Revolutionary war were mellowed down and forgotten under the softening influence of Peace.

FIRST BOOK.

We whose names are hereunto Subscribed Do solemnly and sincerely Declare and Swear, (or affirm,) That the State of Pensilvania is and of right ought to be a free Sovereign and Independent State—and I do forever renounce all Allegiance, Subjection and Obedience to the King or Crown of Great Britain, and I do further swear (or solemnly, sincerely and truely declare and affirm) that I never have since the declaration of Independence, directly or Indirectly aided, assisted, abetted or in any wise countenanced the King of Great Britain, his Generals, fleets or armies; or their adherents in their claims upon these United States, and that I have ever since the declaration of the Independence thereof demeaned myself as a faithfull citizen and subject of this or some one of the United States, and that I will at all times maintain and support the freedom, sovereignty and Independence thereof.

1778.
Decr. 11, HENRY SCHWALBAH.
    12, BENJAMIN LOXLY, JUNR., late a prisoner in Europe.
    14, DAVID JONES, Farmer.
    15, JOHN CROWDEN (his mark), of Philada., Labourer.
        JOHN WEYANT.
    16, JOHN STONE.
        ADAM HUBLEY, of Philada., Mercht.
        JACOB HARMAN, of Philada., Mercht. Affirmed.
        JAMES MCGILL (his mark), do. Labourer.

1778.

Decr. 18, JOHN NIXON,
J. M. NESBITT, } Auditors of Accounts.
BENJ. FULLER,

BARTHOLOMEW MOORE, Mariner, lately in the State fleet.

19, ABRAHAM LEVERING, Roxborough.   Affirmed.
JACOB GILBERT, JUNR.
JACOB GILBERT, the elder.
CASPAR SAUDER.

21, MICHAEL ORNER, Labourer.
ANDREW BRAND, Grocer.
LEONARD KROMER, Northern Liberties.
EVERHART GEISS (his mark), Northern Liberties.
JOHN RIGHTER, Roxborough.

22, BENJAMIN PASCHALL, ESQ. Affirmed.
ROBERT JEWELL.   Affirmed.
CHARLES BOWER, sworn Dec. 24th.
JOSEPH REED, President of the Executive Council.
GEORGE BRYAN, Vice President.
JOSEPH HART,
JOHN MACKY,
MATTHEW SMITH, } Members of the Supreme Executive Council.
JAMES READ,
JACOB ARNDT,
THOMAS SCOTT,

TIMOTHY MATLACK, Secy. of the Council. Affirmed.

25, DANIEL RIGHTER, Roxborough.
MICHAEL RIGHTER,   do.
JOHN RIGHTER,   do.
JAMES HORNER, of Philada., Sadler.

1778.
Decr. 27, JOSEPH STRETCH, of Philada., Mercht. Affirmed.
SAMUEL LANGDALE, do. do. do.
GEORGE CHANDLER, of do. Escort. do.
WILLIAM MATLACK, do. Watchmaker. do.
28, ANDREW DOZ, Philada., Gent.
30, JACOB CONRAD, JR. (his mark), Lower Merrion.
1779.
Jan. 1, FREDERICK SEEGEZ, Shopkeeper.
SAMUEL LYON, Commissary.
JAMES DUNLAP, Philada., Physician.
2, PETER CRISPIN, Roxbury.
JOHN TIBIN, JR., do.
JOSEPH LEAMAN (his mark), do.
MICHAEL SMITH (his mark), Merrion. Farmer.
WILLIAM KIDD, Schoolmaster.
4, PHILIP RUMBLE (his mark), Labourer.
MICHAEL METZINGER (his mark), Weaver.
5, NICHOLAS JACOBS, Cordwainer.
WILLIAM LAWRENCE, Hatter. Affirmed.
PHILIP TRUCKENMILLER, Taylor.
JONATHAN DRAPER, Cordwainer.
JOHN GARDNER, do.
MARTIN BENNER (his mark).
PETER SUTTER, Hatter.
GEORGE ATTKINSON, Ship Captain.
ADAM MYRTELUS, Blacksmith.
JACOB ERINGER, of Philada., Hosier.
MILES HILLBORN, Mercht. Affirmed.
ANDREW TYBOUT, Hatter.
LEVY MARKS, Taylor.

1779.
Jan. 5, BARNABY DEMPSEY (his mark), Labourer.
    9, JOHN FRY (his mark), of Abbendon.
       JAMES CLAYPOOLE ESQ., High-Sheriff.
       JOHN KEBLE, Clark.
       RICHARD SALTAR, Shipwright.
       THOMAS VAUGHAN, do.
       NATHANIEL GREEN, do.
       LEWIS HAZLEWANGER (his mark), do.
       CONRAD LUTZ, do.
       JOHN McKIM.
   13, JACOB GRAFF, Philada.
       JACOB BECHER, Lancaster Co.
       JOHN ANDREWS (his mark), Philada., Waterman.
   14, ANDREW MERVINE (his mark), Cooper.
       BENJAMIN LEAVERING (his mark), Cordwainer.
   16, JOHN KELLY, Asst. Bar. Masr., who also took the oath of office.
   18, EDWARD KERAN, of Philada., Scrivener.
   21, JOHN WEAVER, late in the American Military service.
   26, JOSEPH SHRIVER, of Philada., Butcher.
   28, JOHN AMOS, Lower Merrion, Shoemaker.
       JACOB AMOS (his mark), Roxborough.
   29, CHRISTOPHER BAKER.
   30, THOMAS McDOWELL, of Philada., Soapboiler.
Feb. 3, JOSEPH SELLERS, Kingsessing. Affirmed.
    4, WILLIAM HOLLINSHEAD ESQ.
       WILLIAM ALBRECHT, Philada., Barber.
       WENDELL KINGSFIELD, Lower Merrion.
   10, WILLIAM COCHRAN, L. Merrion.

1779.

Feb. 10, JAMES CHRISTY (his mark), of Bucks, on the publick service.
  13, GEORGE FISHER (his mark), Roxbury.
  JOSEPH PRICE, Carpenter. Affirmed.
  16, JOHN BELL, Shoemaker. Affirmed.
  17, PHILIP SYNG, Gentleman.
  18, GEORGE ROSS ESQ., Judge of Admiralty.
  20, JAMES RUSSELL, of Lower Merrion.
  23, WILLIAM DUNTON, late a prisoner.
  JOHN DANIEL, late of Bucks Co.
  24, JOHN CONNER, in the publick service.
  27, THOMAS CANNAN, Breeches maker.
  JOSEPH KENDALL, Physitian. Affirmed.
  MICHAEL SHUBART ESQ., Member of Assembly.
  JOHANN CONRAD BROWN, of Philada., Cordwainer.
March 1, WILLIAM FULLERTON, Lower Merrion, Taylor.
  9, PHILIP ROTH, of Philada., Musitian.
  BENJAMIN GORGAS, Roxborough.
  JOHN GORGAS,   do.
  10, JACOB SHARP, in the publick service.
  ANDREW SHARP (his mark), in the publick service.
  SAMUEL BAKER, Kensington, Shipwright.
  11, FREDERICK HITNER, of Philada., Tanner.
  12, JOHN LODGE, of Passiunk.
  WILLIAM JONES,
  JOSEPH DURLING, } Mariners of the State of Massachusetts.
  JOHN SMITH,
  13, JACOB AMOS, of Roxborough, Philada. Co.
  JACOB FISLER, of Merrion.
  JOHN HOLEGIT, of Roxborough. Affirmed.

1779.
March 13, ANDREW DAMM, of Philada., Dealer.
    JOHN VESTARD (his mark), of Philada., Brickmaker.
    PETER DAVID HANSIL (his mark), of Kingsessing.
19, JOHN ROUKING, of Philada.
20, LAZARUS PINE ESQ., of Philada., Capt. of Militia.
24, ANDREW FITE, of Roxborough.
26, WILLIAM WATKINS,
    JONATHAN PAUL,
    WILLIAM DAVIES,
    PHILIP REFFERT,
    JAMES MCCOTTER,   } belonging to the Company of Artificers.
    LEONARD EGEN,
    JACOB ALBRIGHT,
    ROBERT IRWIN,
    DAVID PAUL,
    JOHN GEORGE FOX SENR.,   do.
    JOHN HARRAWAY,   do.
27, THOMAS BOURNE, of Philada., Gentleman.
    JOHN BIGONY (his mark), of Roxborough, Hosier.
    DAVID RITTENHOUSE ESQ., State Treasurer.
    CORNELIUS HOULGATE, of Roxborough. Affirmed.
    JOSEPH BIGONY,   do.
    MATTHEW HOLEGET,   do.   Affirmed.
    JOSEPH STURGIS,   do.   do.
    JACOB LUTCH (his mark), Lower Merrion, Cordwainer.
29, PETER TAYLOR, of Philada, Carpenter.
    JACOB CONROD (his mark), of Lower Merrion.
    THOMAS NEVELL,
    JACOB SCHREINER,   } Street Commissioners.
    JOHN MCCULLOH,

1779.
March 29, GEORGE DUNHOWER (his mark), Kingsessing.
    CHRISTOPHER ELLIOTT,   do. Affirmed.
    JOHN FAJON, of Roxborough.
    JOHN WALTERS, Kingsessing.
    ISAAC GRANT,   do.
    ROBERT RIGG, of the Company of Carpenters.
    WILLIAM ROSE,   do.
  30, WILLIAM CHAIN, of Philada., Tallow Chandler.
    NEELS JONASSON,   of Kingsessing.
    FREDERICK HOLSTEN,   do.
    MATTHIAS HOLSTEN,   do.
    JOHN MATZINGER (his mark),   do.
  31, JACOB HAASS, of Philada. Co., of the Co. of Carpenters.
    WILLIAM FIANS, Kingsessing.
    ISRAEL MORTON,   do.
    STOKELY HOSSMAN.
    (HON.) JOHN HAMBRIGHT, Mem. of Ex. Council.
    REUBEN HALL, Philada., Carpenter.
    MARTIN MILLER, Lower Merrion. Affirmed.
    JOHN GOODMAN,   do.   do.
    JACOB CASTER, Oxford.
    HENRY KATZ, Whitemarsh.
    JACOB LAUGHLIN,
    GEORGE SCHLOSSER,
    WILLIAM RUSH,   } County Assessors.
    CHRISTIAN SCHNEIDER,
    ROBERT CURRY,
    WILLIAM RICHARDS, Asst. Assessor.
    WILLIAM GREENWAY, Measurer of Grain.

1779.

March 31, BENJAMIN PASCHALL, Kingsessing. Affirmed.
PAUL CONNER, Roxborough. Affirmed.
RUDOLPH LATCH, Lower Merrion.
JOSEPH STILES, Commissary of Mil. Stores. Affirmed.
GEORGE BELL, Darby Township.
EDWARD PRICE. Affirmed.
GEORGE MORTON, Kingsessing.
ABRAHAM HOLMES, Darby.
SAMUEL TAYLOR, Kingsessing.
SAMUEL YOUNG, Philada., Carpenter.
GEORGE JANUS, D. M., Philada.
ROBERT TOWERS JUNR., Philada., Cutler.
JOHN HENDERSON, of Philada., Conducr. Mil. Stores.
CHRISTIAN BEACKLEY, Philada., Supt. Artificers.
DAVID DAVIES, Comp. Artificers.
RUDOLPH SIBLEY (his mark), Lower Merrion.
PETER HOLSTEN, Kingsessing.
PETER ROSE, Blockley.
JACOB ROWAND, of Philada., Shoemaker.
HENRY SHOSTER, Lower Merrion.
GUNNING BEDFORD, Philada., Carpenter.
GEORGE GROTZ, of Philada., Breeches Maker.

April 7, (DOCTR.) ALVERY HODGSON, Surgeon Genl. Hospital.
ROBT. WILSON, late of New Jersey, now of Philada., Mercht.
JACOB LEVERING, of Roxborough.
13, HENRY MCGEE (his mark), of Philada., Labourer.
14, JOSIAH GILL, of Philada., Shop Keeper. Affirmed.

1779.
April 24, SETH WILLIS, of Philada.
  28, EVAN MORRIS, of Philada., Shoemaker.
  29, JAMES DAVIS, of Merrion, Schoolmaster.
May 4, JOHN DUMFIELD (his mark), a non resident, late of the Jersey State.
  5, JOHN ROBERTS, of Lower Merrion, Farmer. Affirmed.
   SEBASTIEN HOUSHOLD (his mark), a non resident.
  7, ANDREAS FISHER (his mark), of Blockley, Farmer.
  10, THOMAS CARTER, of Philada., Taylor.
  13, THOMAS HALE, Agent for forfeited estates, who also took the oath of said office.
  15, WILLIAM MCSPARRAN, of Philada., Spinner.
   JOHN HORN, of Philada., Spinner.
  22, PETER STOUT, of Philada., Labourer.
   PHILIP CLAUZER (his mark), do. do.
  24, WILHELM FRIEDERICH, of Passyunk, Farmer.
  25, GEORGE YOUNG, of Moyamensing, Farmer.
   HUGH COLVIN (his mark), late of Chester Co., in the publick service.
   ANDREW LEMAU, of Philada., Harness Maker.
   CONRAD SHALLER,
   PHILIP YOUNG,
   HEINRICH LENTZ,
   JOHANNES RITIGER,
   } Having renounced allegiance to the English, which they were constrained to take.
  26, BASTIA VENIA (his mark).
   JOSEPH MEYER,
   JACOB KEISLER (his mark),
   } Moyamensing Farmers.
  27, (Mr.) P. E. DU SIMITIERE, of Philada., Gentleman.
   LUDWIG TAYLOR, Northern Liberties, Cutter.

1779.
May 27, JOHN DANIEL, of Philada.
    JOHN CORBRIGHT, do.
    28, JAMES STURGIS, of Blockley, Weaver.
    HENRY GIBBONS (his mark), of Philada., Labourer.
    29, HENRY THIELL, of Philada., Blacksmith.
    31, JOHN YOUNG, lately residing in the Jersey State.
    WM. RUSK, of Philada., late Butcher.
    ANDREW WAY, of Philada., Taylor.
June 2, GEORG BECHTEL, of Philada., Labourer.
    WILLIAM WRIGHT, of Philada., Sailmaker.
    3, JOHN MALONE (his mark), of Philada., Taverner and Huxter.
    9, VALENTINE HASIG, of Roxbury, Labourer.
    12, WILLIAM HANSELL, Philada., Blacksmith.
    19, HUGH MITCHELL, Clark to Col. Mitchell.
    JOHN MURGATROYD, of Philada., Merchant.
    23, HENRY HART (his mark), of the City Watch, took the test in 1777.
    GEORGE HART (his mark), of the City Watch, testified in 1777.
    JOSEPH HARVEY, late of Bermuda.
    WILLIAM SLOAN, of Cranbury, New Jersey.
    JAMES THOMPSON, of Essex Co., New Jersey.
July 8, JOHN STARKE, of Philada., Wheelwright. Took the test to the States in 1777 & was constrained to Allegiance to the Brittish.
    JOHN BRITTIN, of New Jersey.
    30, SAML. CRAWFORD, of Philada., Mariner.
    JOHN MCCARTNEY, of Philada., Taylor.
    JACOB CHRYSTLER, of Philada., Shopkeeper.

1779.
July 30, EDWARD YOUNG, of Philada., Sadler.
    WILLIAM METAY, of Philada., Sadler.
    31, MATTHEW FOLK, . do. Skindresser.
    PETER HUTMAN (his mark), of Philada., Chairmaker.
    FRANCIS GEISSE, of Philada., Silversmith, took the test in 1777, was constrained to swear to the Brittish when here.
    AMBROSE CROKER, of Philada.
    JAMES LUCAS, Adjutant in the Artillery of Artificers.
    JOHN THORNHILL JUNR., of Philada., Shoemaker.
Aug. 2, GEORGE SWATS, of Philada., Taylor.
    HENRY HYNEMAN (his mark), do. do.
    JOHN LIPPEE (his mark), of Passyunk, Labourer.
    CHRISTIAN CHEVILIER (his mark), do. do.
    JOHN HAY, of Philada.
    JAMES STEEL, of Philada., Gent.
    ISAAC COURSE, do. do.
    CHARLES LOARDAN, took the test in 1777.
    JACOB FACUNDUS, of Philada., Blacksmith.
    DANIEL MORRISON (his mark), of Philada., Labourer.
    JOHN COPPLE (his mark), of Passyunk.
    JOHN BARCLAY, do. Mercht.
    JOHN DOUGLASS, of Passyunk, Linen Printer.
    PETER SMALLWOOD (his mark), Shoemaker.
    JACOB STEINMIRES (his mark), of Philada., Shoemaker.
    JOHN COLLINS, of Philada., Cooper.
    HEINRICH SMALTZ, do. Joyner.
    GEORGE IRONRING (his mark), do. Labourer.
    JOHN MOORE, do. Butcher.

1779.

Aug. 2, MICHAEL STANLEY (his mark), of Philada., Cordwainer.
PEARCE LEWIS, do. do.
JOHN WYANT, of Northern Liberties, Labourer.
JOHN WOOD (his mark), do. do.
GEORGE APT (his mark), do. Pumpmaker.
JAMES CARUTHERS, of Philada., Shopkeeper.
CASPER FLEISHER, do. Skinner.
GEORGE SINK, do. Labourer.
GEORGE HINEY, of Northern Liberties, Labourer.
THOMAS BECK (his mark), City of Philada., Cordwainer.
NICHOLAS HYSMMINGLE, do. Carpenter.
JOHN RIED (his mark), of Northern Liberties, Baker.
CHRISTIAN KIRKHOFF, of Philada., Clark.
ANDREW MCINTIRE, do. Joyner.
DANIEL SHAW, do. Carpenter.
GEORGE HESS, do. Smith.
RICHARD GUY, do. Carpenter.
ROBERT LEECH, do. do.
WILLIAM GRIFFITH (his mark), do. Labourer.
JOHN SPIEGEL, do. Combmaker.
EDWARD DICKENS, do. Painter.
JAMES ROTHBOTTOM, do. Bricklayer.
JOHN GUY, do. Carter.
JOHN BEAKS, do. Carpenter.
GODFREY BACKIUS, do. Hatter.
RICHARD HALL, do. Carpenter.
ABRAHAM AKELY (his mark), do. Cooper.
CONRAD PIGEON, do. Bricklayer.

1779.
Aug. 2, PETER BOYLE (his mark), of Philada., Brewer.
JOHN DEAL, do. Labourer.
JOHN KEYS, do. Hatter.
PETER MELLENBERGER (his mark), do. Labourer.
JONATHAN SMITH, Northern Liberties, Carpenter.
JOSEPH SMITH, Northern Liberties, Saddlemaker.
JOSIAH HAZLETON, Northern Liberties, Smith.
WILLIAM THORN, City, Carpenter.
GEORGE TILL, Northern Liberties, Shipwright.
MICHAEL SHILLING (his mark), City, Combmaker.
WILLIAM POWELL, N. Liberties, Sawyer.
RICHARD TAYLOR, Southwark, Mariner.
JOHN ARMSTRONG (his mark), City, Labourer.
HENRY PERRET, City, Soapboiler.
JOHN PARKHILL, City, Gunsmith.
JAMES HUMPHREYS (his mark), N. Liberties, Shipwright.
JOHN RUTHERFORD, of Philada., Currier.
BENJAMIN BOULTER, do. Carpenter.
JOHN RICE, do. Baker.
NICHOLAS GRIM, do. Sawyer.
JOHN WHITEMAN, do. Taylor.
JOHN WAINE (his mark), do. Labourer.
ANDREW ISINHOOT, N. Liberties, Coppersmith.
HUGH FERGUSON, City, Coachman.
PETER GREEN (his mark), N. Liberties, Currier.
ISAAC CAUSTEN, City, Founder.
FREDERICK GRISLER, do. Innholder.
WILLIAM LOHMAN, Passiunk, Farmer.
WILLIAM BUDDEN, Capt., Philada.

1779.

Aug. 2, GEORGE COOK, inlisted in the Regt. of Artificers.
    MICHAEL FOX, City, Turner.
    JOHN HOFFSTEDLER, City, Cooper.
    JACOB MAAG,   City, Wheelwright.
    SAMUEL STERN,   do. Carpenter.
    JOHN SHAFER,   do. Butcher.
    JOHN McNAIR,   do. Taylor.
    WILLIAM MILLER, do. Printer.
    GEORGE STOW,   do. Turner.
  3, JACOB BOST (his mark), Passiunk, Farmer.
    JACOB SMITH (his mark), do. do.
    GEORGE MOSER (his mark), Kensington, Smith.
    ALEXANDER BARCLAY (his mark), City, Waggoner.
    JOHN QUAIN,   City, at the Laboratory.
  5, JONATHAN CLAY,   do. Blacksmith.
    GEORGE SCHNEIDER,   do. Farmer.
    WILLIAM BAKER (his mark), do. Labourer.
  6, JOHN ANDERSON,   do. Taylor.
  7, ADAM GARRETT (his mark), Passiunk, Farmer.
    EDWARD CARTWRIGHT, late of Philada., Blacksmith.
  9, HENRY SAVETT, of Southwark, Labourer.
10, JOHN McFARLANE, of Philada., late of New York, Mercht.
    JACOB BANKSON the Elder, of Southwark, Yeoman.
    JAMES TAWNEY, of Philada., Travelling Dealer.
18, NICHOLAS MILLER, of do. Labourer.
19, CARL BLUTZER, a Hessian deserter: oath of June 13, 1777.
20, DAVID CROTTY, Seaman, lately discharged from the State Fleet.

1779.
Aug. 20, JOHAN UMBRIGHT, of Philada., Taylor.
TERENCE DONNELLY, of the State of Connecticut.
MICHAEL MÜLLER, of Southwark, Gun Stocker.
RICHARD LUDGATE (his mark), of Philada., Labourer.
23, JAMES HARRIS, do. Cordwainer.
30, SOLOMON TAYLOR, late of Virginia, Blacksmith.
Sept. 3, JOSEPH WEBB, of Philada., House Carpenter. Affirmed.
4, DAVID HANSELL, of Kingsessing, Farmer.
6, JOHN MILLER (his mark), of Philada., Baker. Affirmed.
ANDREW HODGE JUNR., do. absent in the West Indies until November last.
9, MICHAEL LETTS (his mark), of Whitemarsh, Farmer.
ROBERT MILLER, of the N. Liberties, Labourer.
(CAPT.) JOHN LAWSON, of Philada., Mariner.
11, WILLIAM NOLBROW, do. Taylor.
13, ROBERT CORNISH, do. Sailor.
17, JOHN MILLS (his mark), of the N. Liberties, Labourer.
18, ARTHUR HURRY, of Philada., Taylor, now near 19 yrs. of age.
25, GEORGE SNELING (his mark), of Philada., Weaver.
29, CHARLES LOGAN, do. Mercht. Affirmed.
30, JEAN LOUIS REY, late of Geneva, Mercht.
Oct. 4, JAMES HUDSON, of Philada., Sadler and Harness Maker.
WILLIAM WARNER JUNR., of Blockley.
7, WALTER HALL, of Philada., Merchant.
9, JOHN SOLTER, of Philada., Baker.

1779.

Oct. 9, JESSE JONES, of Lower Merrion Township, Philada. co. Affirmed.

11, JOHN ERDMAN SMITH, of Philada., Printer.
CHARLES MERIDITH, do. Gentleman.
ALGERNON ROBERTS.
WILLIAM JACKSON, of Philada., Mercht.

12, ROBERT HEYSHAM, of do. do.
CHARLES STEDMAN, do. Gentleman.
CARPENTER WHARTON, of Southwark, Mercht.
JOHN KESSLER.
JOHN PALMER, of Philada., Tavern keeper.
PETER LIGHT (his mark), Philada., Labourer.
WILLIAM COLLOM (his mark), worker in the Armory, Philada.

Lists of the foregoing returned to Election at State House.

Oct. 13, WILLIAM JONES, of Philada., Grazier.
GEORGE WALKER, do. Victualer.
ABRAHAM SINK (his mark), do. Brassfounder.
PETER RAMBO, do. Sadler.
14, JOSEPH HILLBORN, do. Mercht. Affirmed.
GEORG DAVID SICKEL, do. Butcher.
JAMES CALDWELL, of Northern Liberties, Labourer.
CHARLES KNIGHT, of Philada., Miller.
JOHN DIAMOND, do. Ropemaker.
JAMES ARMSTRONG, do. Trader.
DANIEL BENEZET, do. Mercht.
JOHN BARE, do. Hatter.

1779.
Oct. 14, SAMUEL PENROSE, of Philada., Mercht.
    15, GEORGE DELANEY, Darby,   Seaman.
    16, THOMAS SMITH (his mark), Philada., do.
        JOHN BECK,   do. Taylor.
        JOHN WEAVER,   do. do.
        JOSHUA JONES, Lower Dublin, Philada. co., Farmer.
        ISAAC WHARTON, of Philada., Mercht. Affirmed.
        CHARLES WHARTON, do. do. do.
        JOSEPH HIBBARD, Blockley, Farmer.
        SAMUEL PETERS, Philada., Schoolmaster.
        JOHN HEFFERNAN, do. do.
        JOHN OTENKERKEN, do. Labourer.
    18, JOHN PORTER,   do. Student in Phisick.
        MICHAEL LEIB,   do. do.
        JACOB FRANK,   do. Silversmith.
        PETER KURTZ,   do. Tobacconist.
        GODFREY SHISLER, Passiunk, Farmer.
        JAMES KINNEAR, of Philada., Mercht.
        PETER FOOTMAN, do. do.
        JOHN GROVER,   Lower Merrion, Farmer.
        HEINRICH COLFLESH,   do. do.
        MATHIAS COLFLESH,   do. do.
        JOHANNES WALTERS,   do. do.
        PHILIP PRITNER,   do. do.
        ISRAEL JONES,   do. do. Affirmed.
        THOMAS MORGAN,   do. do. Affirmed.
        ROBERT BASS, Philada.,   Druggist.
        THOMAS GRESWOLD, Northern Liberties. do.

1779.

Oct. 18, JONATHAN ZANE, Northern Liberties, Mercht.
 JOHN CARNS JUNR., Darby, Chester Co., Yeoman.
 EDWARD ELLIOTT, Philada., Clark.
 TENCH FRANCIS, Philada., Gent.
 JOSEPH PALMER, do. Mercht. Affirmed.
 JAMES PEALE, do. Gentleman.
 JOHN YOUNG, Lower Merrion, Gent.
 JOHN STEINMETZ, Philada., do.
 ELEAZER LEVY, late of New York, Trader.
 JOHN FEGAL, Northern Liberties, Shopkeeper.
 JOHN WILLIAMS, Philada., House Carpenter.
19, GEORGE CLAYPOOLE, of Philada., Cabinet Maker.
 ANDREW HAMILTON, of do. Gentleman.
 EDMOND NUGENT, of do. Breeches maker.
 GEORGE FORSYTH, of do. Innholder.
 THOMAS HUMPHREYS, Merrion, Philada. Co., Blacksmith.
 JAMES CARR, do. Weaver.
 LUDWICK KNOLL, do. Farmer.
 JACOB BARE, do. do.
 JOHN BARE, do. do.
 ALEXANDER SOLY, do. Cordwainer.
 CHRISTIAN LAWYER, Philada. Co., Labourer.
 CONROD GOODMAN, Merrion, Philada. Co., Weaver.
 WILLIAM E. GODFREY, Capt. Lieut. Artillery.
 DAVID PANCOAST, Philada., House Carpenter.
 JOHN MCALESTOR, Yorktown, Commissary.
 JOHN FRYHOFFER, Lower Dublin, Phil. Co., Taylor.
 WOLLERY FRYHOFFER, do. Farmer.
 GEORGE RATZNER, do. do.

1779.

Oct. 19, JOSEPH MATHIAS (his mark), Lower Dublin, Farmer.
JEREMIAH LYNN, Co. Philada., Shipwright.
JACOB BAKER, Co. do. Shopkeeper. Affirmed.
REES PRICE, Philada. County, Farmer. Affirmed.
WILLIAM DELLAP, Co. Philada., Trader. Affirmed.
FRANCIS JONES, Philada. County, Gent. Affirmed.
JOHN LLEWELYN, Lower Merrion, Weaver. do.
LLEWELYN YOUNG, do. Farmer. Affirmed.
HENRY PUGH, do. Weaver. do.
MORRISS LLEWELYN, do. House Carpenter. Affirmed.
JOSEPH LOWNES, Co. Philada., Silversmith.
DAVID RIDDLE, do. Saddler.
JOHN DARRACH, do. Saddler.
JOHN BRYAN, do. Saddler.
JOHN CORSE, do. do.
ISAAC PENROSE, do. Mercht.

20, JAMES WINTER, of Lower Merrion, Farmer.
BENJAMIN HOLLAND, do. Weaver.
DAVID ZELL, do. Farmer. Affirmed.
CASPAR WHITEMAN (his mark), do. Farmer.
JOSEPH BEDFORD, Philada., Gentleman.
PETER BEDFORD, do. do.
LAWRENCE POWELL, do. Baker.
WILLIAM TYSON, Blockley, Shoemaker. Affirmed.
MATTHIAS TYSON, Darby, Farmer. Affirmed.
WILLIAM MACKENZIE, of Philada., Mercht.
WILLIAM JEFFERY, Northern Liberties, Labourer.
JAMES DELAPLAINE, Northern Liberties, Taverner.
JACOB GOMINGER, Germantown, Miller. Affirmed.

1779.

Oct. 20, STEPHEN BLUNT, Philada., Shoemaker.
ISAAC LEECH, Cheltenham, Tanner.
JOHN SPEDE, Philada., Baker.
EDMOND FAGAN, N. Liberties, Cordwainer.
MICHAEL MCMULLEN, Lower Merrion, Farmer.
SAMUEL BAKER, N. Liberties, Ship Carpenter.
JOSHUA PEARSON, Co. Philada., Cordwainer. Affd.
WILLIAM FOLLWELL, Philada., Taylor. Affd.
HUGH KNOX, of Philada. County, Farmer.
LEONARD KESSLER, of Philada., Joyner.
ROBERT BELL, do. Printer.
THOMAS CARRADINE, do. late from **Maryland**, Mercht.
GEORGE CLACKNER, of Kingsessing, Taylor.
JOSEPH LEDRA, of Philada., Bricklayer.
JOHN LOHRA, do. now 18 years of **age**. Retailer.
ROBERT CRAIN, made proof that he in March 1778, took the oath to the States before Genl. Green and now before me.

25, JACOB TREN (his mark), of Passiunk, made oath that he in the year 1777 before Justice Young, took the Oath of Allegiance and the foregoing this day.

Dec. 30, JAMES FARNSWORTH, An inhabitant of Philada. in the year 1777, made Oath that in that year he took the Oath of Allegiance to the States before Justice Smithson in the Jersey State and now before me.

1780.

March 6, JOHN M. JACKSON, now of the age of eighteen years and one month, of Philada., Clark.

1780.

May 6, PETER OTT, of Blockley Township, Farmer, having taken the test to the States in 1777, was compelled to swear allegiance to the Brittish while here, much against his will as he declares, and which he most heartily renounces.

JOHN DAW, being a Commissioned Officer in the 4th Pensilvania Regt. in the year 1777.

15, DANIEL APPEL, lately from the West Indies, Taylor.

HOSEA SMITH, lately come of age, Taylor.

June 8, JACOB RICKNEAL (his mark), lately discharged from the German American Regt.

JAMES COTTRINGER, of Philada., Brushmaker, but lately arrived to the age of eighteen years.

12, LUKE MORRIS JUNR., Miller, in his minority. Affirmed.

13, WILLIAM DOUGLASS, taken prisoner under age and lately returned.

Note that DANIEL FOLT, of Passiunk not taking the test in time desired now to take it, which he did and I gave a certificate according thereto.

June 28, DANIEL MCLEAN, a Sergeant in the service of this and of the United States the 1st day of June 1778, and since with reputation discharged.

Sep. 9, JAMES KIRK, a soldier in the service of the American United States on the 1st day of June 1778, and since discharged.

25, WILLIAM DUE (his mark), Mariner, resident in this city above five years, being a foreigner unacquainted with the time prescribed by law.

1780.

Sep. 30, MATTHEW PHELPS, of the state of Connecticut, lately from the Mississippi, Planter.

Oct. 10, ISAAC SHELDON, of the State of Connecticut, lately from the Mississippi, Planter.

ABRAHAM HARGIS, a Lieut. in the Continental Army, 10th Pena. Regt. June 1st, 1778.

ROBERT KENNEDY, from South Carolina, Taylor.

21, NICHOLAS HINKLE (his mark), of Blockley, lived in the Jersey State in the year 1776, where he first proved his allegiance.

Dec. 5, PHILIP SWARTZ, charged with treasonable practices and discharged after a long confinement. Recommended by J. C., Sheriff.

13, JOHN ALLEN, of the state of N. Carolina.

1781.

Jan. 29, JOHN COOK (his mark), late of the Jersey state; in Jany. 1779, was qualified to allegiance there before Lemuel Sears in Gloucester County as appears by certificate.

June 14, JOHN JOHNSTON (his mark), by trade a painter and Glazier but has followed the sea some years.

29, JOHN FRAZER (his mark), late a soldier in the Pennsylvania line.

Sep. 7, SAMUEL HEMBEL, formerly a servant in Lancaster co., lately free.

Oct. 8, JAMES HAMPDEN THOMSON, late a citizen of South Carolina and lately arrived in this city from St. Augustine.

9, ADAM GILCHRIST, an officer in the Penna. Line in 1777.

1781.
Oct. 9, GEORGE BOND.
    JOHN PHILE, late a free citizen of Maryland, now of this City, Mercht.
    CHARLES PETTIT.
    JAMES WILLING.
    JAMES MONTGOMERY.
    FRANCIS DONNELLY.
    D. WITHERSPOON.
    WILLIAM HENDERSON.
    WILLIAM GRAHAM, late of Virginia.
  13, BENJ. SMITH (his mark), of Blockley Township, Philada. Co.
Nov. 2, JAMES DUFFY (his mark), now City Constable, Philada.
  21, ANDREW MILLER, of Towamensing, Philada. Co., Farmer.
  20, WILLIAM BELL, of Philada., Taylor, late of the State of New Jersey.

1782.
Feb. 16, THOMAS LAKE, son of Capt. Thomas Lake; now 18 years old.
    JOHN FESMORE (his mark), late discharged from the Penna. Line.
Apl. 15, ELEAZER OSWALD, late Lieut. Col. of Arty. of the United States.
May 1, ARCHIBALD MCCLAREY, formerly a private in the river fleet.
  13, BEDFORD WILLIAMS, Surgeon, formerly in the service of the States.
  31, ABRAHAM SEIXAS, formerly an officer in the Militia

1782.

of Charlestown, South Carolina, lately arrived in this city, Mercht.

July 1, WILLIAM BRADFORD, formerly a soldier in the Virginia line, discharged, by trade a Taylor.

13, JOSEPH HELLER, of Merrion Township, lately arrived to the age of 20.

JACOB SIBLEY, of Merrion Township, but lately arrived to the age of 19.

Aug. 7, PHILIP SMITH, a German, bred in Philada., a Taylor by trade.

14, JONATHAN ADAMS, a native of Maryland, by trade a silversmith.

22, MATTHEW BALLAM, a native of New York who retired on the approach of the enemy.

Sep. 14, LEVIN LANGRALL, of the State of Maryland, taken prisoner and escaped from New York, Mariner.

21, ROBERT PATTISON, of Charlestown in South Carolina, Mercht.

Oct. 7, THOMAS STEEL, of Philadelphia, Mariner.

PHILIP MOORE, of Philada., Mercht., having taken the Oath of Allegiance in Boston in 1777 and in the Court of Philada. in April 1782.

JOHN OGDEN, lately arrived to the age of twenty-one years.

JOHN STAFFORD, belonging to the train of Artillery in 1776. Discharged.

JOHN JONES, Health Officer, took the test in Virginia in 1777.

BENJAMIN STAGG, a private in the 5th Penna. Regt. in 1776, discharged in 1781.

1782.

Oct. 7, MICHAEL CONNOR, took the Oath at Reading in June 1778.

DAVID PORTER, an officer in the Penna. Line in 1777.

CHARLES MCCARTER, Surgeon in the 4th Penna. Regt. in 1777.

JAMES MCLEAN, an officer in the Penna. Line in 1777.

LAZARUS STOW, Lieut. in the 11th Penna. Regt. in 1777.

8, JAMES WHITEHEAD.

CHARLES DARRAGH.

MATTHEW MCGUIRE.

WILLIAM GRAY.

ALEXANDER POWER.

JOHN THOMPSON.

JOSEPH RICE.

WILLIAM WILLIAMS.

DAVID ELLIOTT.

PATRICK OWENS, took the test in Virginia in 1777.

JOHN COWELL, surgeon in the Genl. Hospital of Penna. in June 1778.

PATRICK DUFFY, an officer in the Penna. Artillery in 1777.

JOHN KAWORTH, a seafaring man.

JAMES HAMEL, tavern keeper, took the test in Virginia in 1777.

JOHN STRICKER, an officer in the Penna. Line in 1777.

ROBERT SCOT, took the test in Virginia in 1777.

1782.

Oct. 8, JAMES GILCHRIST, an officer in the Penna. Line 1779.
ANDREW LYTLE, an officer in do. 1776.
JOHN BAKER, who took the oath in Virginia, August 1777.
JAMES G. HERRON, late an officer in Hazen's Regiment, Pennsylvania Line.
GEORGE HOFNER, late an officer in the Penna. Line.
JOHN HUNN, took the test in Delaware State 1778.

18, JOHN LOGE, late of Salem, in the State of N. Jersey. Waterman.

Nov. 4, GARRET PETERS, an inhabitant of this City. Shoemaker.

8, ROBERT SMOCK, late of the State of N. Jersey. Clark in the Clothier's Departmt.

19, JOHN BRYARLY, some time resident in this city. Sadler.
WILLIAM PATTON, formerly of Lancaster, in this State. Sadler.
JOHN STILES, some time resident in this city. Sadler.

1783.

Jan. 6, SETH AVERED, from Connecticut, last from Chester Co.

Mch. 19, ANDREW AITKIN, of Philada. Physitian in the Publick service above four years.

April 22, JOHN JAMISON, of Philada. Sadler. Nineteen years of age.

30, GEORGE MAYER, son of Jacob Mayer; a native of Philada., late a prisoner with the enemy, now 19 years old.

May 7, HUGH MARTIN, a surgeon in the Penna. Line in 1778.

1783.

May 30, ADAM STELLER, Butcher, born in Philada., lately of age.

THOMAS BELL, late apprentice to Geo. Claypoole, Cabinet maker.

June 30, GEORGE TUDOR, a Major in the Penna. Line.

PHILIP LAUER, having served five years in the Penna. regiment of Artillery.

Sept. 17, JAMES CHRYSTIE, Captain in the Penna. Line.

JOHN BRICE, formerly Captain in the Marine of this State.

Oct. 6, ABRAHAM HOWELL, of Maurice County, State of New Jersey.

10, JOSEPH HARMA, Lieut. Col. 1st Regt. of Pennsylvania.

PHILIP MENTGES, Lieut. Col. in the Southern Army.

J. MOORE, Major 1st Penna. Regiment.

JOHN BRYCE, Captain Co. of Artillery.

13, WILLIAM MARTIN, Captain of Artillery.

ROBERT WALLACE, proves by certificate that he took the oath of allegiance in the Jersey State in 1777.

14, EDWARD WHELAN, a soldier in the Penna. line. Discharged.

ROBERT MORRELL, an artificer in the American Army. Discharged.

JOHN PATTON, tallow chandler, a native, lately come of age.

JOHN RHEA, of Philada., a native, lately arrived to age.

SAMUEL BRADY, Captain 3rd Penna. Regt.

1783.

Oct. 14, THOMAS ADAMS, late of Rhode Island, made oath that he took the test of that State in 1777.

PAUL JONES, Captain in the Navy of the United States.

JOHN SMITH, late Sergt. in the Penna. Line. Discharged January 1781.

RICHARD WALLACE (his mark), a private in the Penna. Line. Discharged 1781.

JOHN ADAMS, late a sergeant in the Penna. Line. Discharged Jan. 1781.

THOMAS LAVISYLER, late Ensign in the Penna. Line. Deranged.

ISAAC B. DUNN, Capt. 3rd Regt. Penna.

JAMES FINLEY, makes oath that he in 1777, in Virginia, took the oath of that State of his allegiance.

JOHN HAZLEWOOD, JUNR., lately arrived to the age of 21 years.

CHRISTOPHER KUGLER, of the Northern Liberties, but now arrived to 21 years of age.

L. KEENE, late Captain 2nd Penna. Regt.

EPHRAIM BLAINE, Commissary General Purveyor.

JOHN READ.

ALEXANDER RUSSELL, late Lieut. 7th Penna. Regt.

ALEXANDER BENSTED, late Lieut. & Paymaster 10th Penna. Regt.

THOMAS MCINTIRE.

MARTIN WEYLAND, of Point no Point Northern Liberties, maketh oath which is certified to by Edward Pool, in 1778.

HENRY GREVE, Lieut. in the 4th Penna. Regt.

1784.
Oct. 11, JOHN WHITE, Mate of the General Military Hospital.
12, ROBERT GREGG, late Captain of the Penna. Line.
JACOB COX, made oath that he took the oath of allegiance in the Jersey State in 1777.
JNO. DONOHUE, made oath that he gave test of allegiance in the Jersey State, and since agreeable to law in this State.
WILLIAM HONEYMAN, formerly a lieut. in the Pensyla. Line.
WILLIAM NORTON, formerly a private in the Pena. Line. Discharged.
MATTHEW MCCLENTICK, took the oath in Maryland in 1780.
PATRICK SHAW (his mark), a private in the Penna. Line. Discharged.

1785.
Feb. 19, ISAAC VAN VLECK, of the Jersey State, appears to have taken the oath of allegiance in that State in 1777.
Apl. 11, EDWARD TILGHMAN, JUNR., of Dover, in the Delaware State, Esq., appears to have taken the oath of allegiance in said State.
Sep. 29, FRANCIS KNOX, Commander of a Vessel under commission in the American Service in the late war.
JAMES LOCKWOOD, a native of Connecticut, a resident here near two years. Mercht.
Oct. 6, JOHN MITCHELL, of Philada. Mercht.
JOHN SAVIDGE, a Captain in the Pensilva. Line in 1778.
PHILIP KLEIN, appears to have taken the oath in

1785.

1778; served in the flying camp, and now before me hath taken the oath.

Oct. 6, JOHN ORGAN (his mark), late a soldier in the Pensyla. Line six years.

JOHN MCILENCH (his mark), a soldier in the Pensyla. Line in 1777.

PHILIP COLEWATER (his mark), a soldier in the Pena. Line six years.

24, BARNABY SCULLY, a soldier in the Maryland Line in 1777, since a resident here.

WILLIAM SPOTTSWOOD, from Ireland, resident here about 2 years. Did not take the oath of 1777.

MATTHEW CAREY, from Dublin, Printer, resident here near one year. Did not take the oath of 1777.

1786.

Apl 7, WILLIAM BANKSON, of Philada. Upholsterer, a native of this State, lately arrived to full age.

May 10, ANDREW REY, formerly an officer in the service of the United States, and latterly a resident of the Delaware State.

Oct. 10, DANIEL GARHART (his mark), late a soldier in the American Army, from the commencement of the war.

HENRY LIPSEY, late a soldier in the Artillery of Penna.

HENRY MCANALLY, proves that he took the oath in 1778 before Justice Adcock.

JOSEPH CRAWFORD (his mark), proves that he took the test of 1778 in due time.

1786.
Oct. 10, HENRY HARRIS (his mark), proves that he took the oath of 1778 before me in due time.

1787.
Apl. 5, JOSEPH ANDERSON (ESQ.), Attorney at Law, formerly a Major in the Army of the United States and the Jersey Line.

13, WILLIAM MONTGOMERY (ESQ.), Attorney at Law, formerly a Citizen of the Delaware State.

SECOND BOOK.

We the subscribers do swear (or affirm) that I renounce and refuse all allegiance to George the third, King of Great Britain, his heirs and successors, and that I will be faithful, and bear true allegiance to the commonwealth of Pensylvania as a free and Independant State, and that I will not at any time do or cause to be done any matter or thing that will be prejudicial or injurious to the freedom and Independance thereof, as declared by Congress; and, also, that I will discover and make known to some one Justice of the Peace of this State, all treasons or traitorous conspiracies which I now know or hereafter shall know, to be formed against this or any of the United States of America.

PLUNKETT FLEESON.

Philadelphia, 1778.

1778.
July 11, JAMES HALL.
  JAMES THOMPSON.
  JOHN RIGHTER.
  JOHN KOOK.
 14, JOHANN CHRISTOPHER JUTTER.
  JOHANN CONRAD GOTTHART.
  GEORGE SHARSWOOD.
  JOHN CROOK.
  LUKE KEATING. 2d Certificate proved.
  JOHN PATTERSON.

1778.
July 14, JOHN C. KUNZE.
 15, JOHN HALBURTAT. A 2d Certificate.
  THOMAS HALL. 2d Certificate proved.
  WILLIAM ROBINSON.
  GEORGE CROGHAN.
 20, JOHAN GEORG MILLER.
  ROBERT BASS.
  WILLIAM MATLACK. Affirmed.
  WILLIAM PUGH. Affirmed.
  CHRISTIAN HANSMAN.
  CHRISTOPHER BAKER.
  JOHN BURNES.
  THOMAS BECK. 2d Certificate.
  PASTORIOUS WYNN. 2d Certificate.
 23, WILLIAM JONES.
  CALEB ASH. Affirmed.
  GEORGE STOCKHAM.
 24, ANDREW BRAND. 2d Certificate.
  GEORGE BATES. do.
  ADAM CLAMPFFER. do.
  JACOB FISLER.
 25, JACOB CARRICK (his mark).
  JACOB CONROD (his mark).
  JACOB LATCH (his mark).
  SAMUEL TOM (his mark).
  GEORGE KURTZ, sworn to have taken the oath of allegiance the 30th June 1777. 2d Certificate.
  FRANCIS FINLEY. 2d Certificate.
  GEORGE FOX.
 27, NN. SELLERS.

1778.

July 27, FRIEDERICH PLACK, swore that he took the test and had a certificate from me in June 1777. 2d Certificate.

JAMES NEILL. Affirmed.

WILLIAM BARNS.

JOHN CUMMINGS.

CONRAD DEWETTER, attests having taken the oath and had my certificate the 26th day of June 1777.

28, JOHN BROWN, Cabinet maker, testifies that on or about the latter end of June 1777, he took the oath, and had my certificate. 2nd Certificate.

WILLIAM MOORE.

JOHN SMITH, of Philada. Breeches maker, sworn, that about the end of June 1777, he took the oath of allegiance, and had a certificate from me, which he hath lost, and now has a 2nd certificate.

29, REES PRICE. Affirmed.

30, WILLIAM STROUD. Affirmed.

JOHN COFFMAN.

GEORGE WOOD.

MATTHIAS NONVELLER, of Blockly, attests to having in June 1777, taken the test, and had my certificate, which he hath lost. 2d Certificate.

JACOB BEALERT, of Blockly, attests to having in June 1777, or thereabout, taken the oath of allegiance, and that he had my certificate, which he hath lost. 2d Certificate.

THOMAS WATTS.

31, GEORGE CHANDLER.

1778.
July 31, ELIJAH COFFIN.   2d Certificate.
    JAMES HARRIS.
    RICHARD PRICE.   Affirmed.
Aug. 1, THOMAS IRWIN.
    W. HAMILTON.
    JACOB ASH, Attests having taken the test with me about June 1777.   2nd Certificate.
    PHILIP CONRAD, Attests to have taken the test about July, 1777.
    MARTIN WALTER.
    WILLIAM MCELVAIN.
  3, PETER CRASS (his mark), Attests to have taken the test in or about the Month of July 1777.
    JONATHAN DRAPER.
    JOHN CORMAN.
    EDWARD RICHIE.
    RUDOLPH SIBLEY (his mark).
    WILLIAM WHITTINGTON, of Boston.
    JOHN OVERLY, Copy from ye Original Sept. 12th 1777. No. 887.
    RICHARD HUNT, Attests to have taken the Test of me in July 1777, & now has a 2d Certificate.
  4, GUNNING BEDFORD.
    GEORGE CLAYPOOLE.
    JOHN KEICHLER (his mark).
    ISAAC WIDDOS, Attests to have taken the Oath & to have lost his Certificate taken in June 1777. 2d Certificate.
    JOHN WEAVER.
    CHARLES CECIL, lately arrived from Europe.

1778.
Aug. 4, JOHN DAVIS. Affirmed.
    5, ISAAC WARNER, did take the test in 1777; was constrained to swear allegiance to the King, which he now doth renounce. 2d Certificate.

       ARCHIBALD MCKENDRICK, a Brittish officer, discharged from parole, and recommended.

       LUDWICK KNOLL.

       CONROD GOODMAN. Affirmed.

       DARBY SAVAGE.

       RICHARD TOPLIFF, Copy from Original June 13 1777. No. 32.

    6, JAMES SPINKS.

       FRIEDERICH DESHONG, took the oath to the States in 1777, was after constrained to swear allegiance to the crown, which he now renounces, and again takes the test to the States. 2d Certificate.

       JACOB LITCHENHAM (his mark).

       BENJAMIN THAW.

    7, LUDWIG FALKENSTEIN.

       PETER REMENDER (his mark).

       SAMUEL EVANS. Affirmed.

       SAMUEL LANGDALE.

       ARCHIBALD WATSON (his mark).

    8, JAMES DAVIS.

       WILLIAM SAUNDERS, Attests to have Attested in July 1777. 2nd Certificate.

       HUGH ROSS, Attests to have taken & subscribed in July 1777. 2d Certificate.

   10, JOHN DIAMOND.

       JACOB ERRINGER.

1778.
Aug. 10, JOHANNES HELLER.
 CHARLES STOW.
 CHRISTOPHER HART (his mark), took the test from me in June 1777, per qualification. 2nd Certificate.
 EDWARD MCDONNELL.
 JOSEPH GOVETT.
 JAMES PACKER. Affirmed.
 JOHN ALLEN (his mark), gunsmith. 2nd Certificate.
 JOHN YERGER.
 JOSEPH WILLIAMSON.
11, THOMAS FLEESON, A 2nd certificate 17th July, 1777.
 MELCHOIR NUFF, taken in Augt. 1777. 2d Certificate.
 SAMUEL STERN.
12, THEOBALD ENT, Sadler, Attested taking in June 1777. 2d Certificate.
 ADAM GROFF (his mark).
 JAMES RUSSELL.
 JOHN HEYL, Attests to having taken the Oath in June 1777. 2nd Certificate.
 PHILIP WARNER, known to have taken the oath in June 1777. 2d Certificate.
 BENJAMIN HUMPHREYS. Affirmed.
 JOSEPH LEONARD. Affirmed.
13, JOHN DAVID.
 RICHARD ROBINSON, who farther attests to have taken the Oath before George Brian, Esq., about the month of July 1777, but lost his Certificate. 2d Cert.

1778.
Aug. 14, WILLIAM SOWERSBY.
WILLIAM LAKE, renewed his Certificate 27th Augt. 1777. No. 850. 2nd Certificate.
GEORGE CONNELL, Carver, renewed his Certificate of 28th June 1777. No. 194. 2d Cert.
DAVID RICHARDS, Affirms to have taken the test on or about July 1777. Renewed his Certificate.
WILLIAM GUINEY.
JACOB BAKER.
15, EDWARD CAVANAUGH (his mark).
WILLIAM ROBINSON.
JACOB HANKEL, Took the test before me about Augt. 1777.
CORNELIUS BARNES.
PETER MELLEN.
THOMAS ROUE.
17, WILLIAM THOMSON.
THOMAS PALMER.
JOSEPH LISLE.
ROBERT DAVIDSON, Took the test in the Delaware State the 2d of June 1778.
JACOB KINNARD.
JACOB BURKLAE.
18, JAMES RASBOTHAM.
ROBERT MOORE, Proves having taken the test of John Crugh, Esq., of Carlisle, which he hath lost. Now taken of me. 2d Certificate.
JOHN REILEY JUNR., Attests to have in 1777 taken test to the States, in Maryland, and lost his certificate.

F

1778.
Aug. 18, GEORGE YOUNG.
    ROBERT BELL. 2d Certificate.
    JOHANNES HILARIUS BAKER.
19, JAMES UNDERWOOD, Affirms to having taken the test & had my certificate in or about Augt. 1777.
    PHILIP YOUNG (his mark).
    RICHARD SINGELTON.
    SIMON HUFTY.
    JOHN COTTMAN.
    THOMAS MORGAN. Affirmed.
    WILLIAM CLARK. Affirmed.
20, GERARD WILLIAM BEEKMAN, 2d Certificate & abjurations.
    THOMAS THOMPSON.
    WILLIAM GRAHAM, known to have taken the test in June 1777, No. 92, Copy.
21, ROBERT PLUNKET.
    JOHN ARMITAGE, took the test in July 1777. 2d Certificate.
22, JACOB BARR.
    JOHN LEAR (his mark).
    JOHN ROBERTS. Affirmed.
    SAMUEL JUNKIN.
    NICHOLAS RICE.
    GEORGE MATZINGER.
    EVAN GRIFFITH.
    FRANCIS JONES. Affirmed.
    CHRISTIAN WORTZHEISER.
    GABRIEL KORN, proves to have taken in July 1777.

1778.

Aug. 24, JOHN LONG, proves having taken the Oath in July 1777.

    MATTHEW FOY, proves to have taken of me about July 1777.

    WILLIAM KEMBLE.

    WILLIAM MOORE.

    WILLIAM DOMILLER (his mark).

25, JOHN GRAVEL, proves to have taken the Oath in July 1777.

    JAMES DEXTER, proves to have taken the Oath in June 1777. 2d Certificate.

    GEORGE LORDEN, proves to have taken the Oath in July, 1777.

26, WILLIAM BEALE.

    WILLIAM TUSTIN.

    WILLIAM TREMPOR, proves having taken the Oath in or about July, 1777.

    DANIEL HARAR.

    JOSEPH SELLERS. Affirmed.

    ADAM METTS, proves having taken the Oath in Augt. 1777.

    JOHN FORD, proves having taken the Oath in July 1777.

    WILHELM BASTIAN.

    THOMAS FITZGERALD, proves that he took the Oath on 30th of June 1777.

    THOMAS FRANCIS, at the same time, and now has his first Certificate. No. 426.

    JOHN VANNOST.

1778.
Aug. 27, CHRISTOPHER REID, swore that he took the test in June 1777.
JOHN HENDERSON.
THOMAS PASCHALL.
JOSEPH HILLBORN.

We the Subscribers do swear (or affirm) that I renounce and refuse all allegiance to George the Third, King of Great Britain, his heirs and successors, and that I will be faithful and bear true allegiance to the Commonwealth of Pensylvania as a free and Independent State; and that I will not at any time do or cause to be done, any matter or thing, that will be prejudicial or injurious to the freedom and Independence thereof, as declared by Congress; and, also, that I will discover and make known to some one Justice of the Peace of the said state all treasons or traitorous conspiracies which I now know or hereafter shall know to be formed against this or any of the United States of America.

PLUNKET FLEESON.

Philadelphia, 1778.

1778.
Aug. 27, JOHN LENNERD, Weaver.
  28, JOHN THOMAS, Also proves to have taken the Oath from Justice Davis, of Chester Co., in 1777.
  MICHAEL DITRICH.
  JACOB RENNO, proves to have taken the Oath in July, 1777.
  JOSEPH PARKES, proves to have taken the Oath in Augt. 1777.
  JOHN BROOKES, proves that he had taken the Oath June 28th 1777.

1778.

Aug. 28, JOHN PALMER, proves to have taken the Oath in June 1777.

THOMAS CRAIG, proves to have taken the Oath on or about Augt. 1777.

STEPHEN SIMONS, proves to have taken the Oath in Jany. 1777.

WILLIAM PINTON, proves taking the Oath in June 1777.

29, JACOB WHITMAN.

FELIX BENTLEY.

GEORGE KOOPER (his mark), proves that he took the test in 1777, & now before me renounces the allegiance extorted by the Brittish.

WILLIAM MCMICHAEL, proves taking the test in July, 1777.

CONRAD STOLTZ, renounces the Allegiance sworn to the Brittish, and taken by force last winter.

CHRISTOPHER MILLER, renounces as above.

EDMOND NUGENT.

31, EDMOND BEECH JUNR., Copy of original July 1st 1777.

JOHN MARTIN, proves to have taken the test in Augt. 1777.

JOSEPH PEMBERTON.

HOYMON LUY, proves that he did take the test in Augt. 1777.

JAMES OELLERS, proves that in June 1777 he did take the test, but was constrained to Brittish Allegiance, and this day renews his Allegiance to the State.

1778.

Sept. 2, ABRAHAM GLOEDING, proves to have taken the test in June 1777.
CHRISTIAN PETERMAN.
GEORGE MAKEMSON.

3, HENRY CRESS, proves to have taken the test to the United States in 1777; was constrained to Brittish Allegiance, and this day renounces the latter & swears allegiance to the United States.
FRANCIS BOWER, swears to have taken the test in 1777 before Justice Hull, of Connecocheque, and now before me.
COOPER BRETHOWER, proves to have taken the test in Augt. 1777.

4, MICHAEL CLARK, sworn to have taken the test to the State in July 1777.
ENNION WILLIAMS, proves to have taken the test of me in June, 1777.
JONATHAN HEATON.

5, ANTHONY KIRK (his mark).
CASPER SOUDER, took the test in June 1777; has since been constrained to swear allegiance to the Brittish, and this day renews his first oath.

7, THOMAS RENSHAW, proves to have taken the State test in June, 1777. No. 17. 2nd Certificate. Affirmed.
JOHN TOMKINS.
JOHN EVERLY (his mark).

8, WILLIAM DAVIDSON, a prisoner and on parole, from the 16th of November to this time.
BARTHOLOMEW THAYER.

1778.
Sept. 8, JOSEPH HIBBERD.
    SAMUEL PENROSE.
  9, THOMAS WELCH. Affirmed.
    JOSEPH HONEYCOMB, proves to have taken the State test in 1777.
    MATTHEW HOOPER, proves to have taken the State test in June 1777.
    JOHN COATES, proves that he took the State test in June 1777.
    JOSEPH BOLTER, proves that he took the State test in June 1777.
    IMANUEL JACOB ALBORN.
  11, JAMES MURDAUGH.
    EDWARD FLOUNDERS, proves to have taken the test of me in August 1777. Affirmed.
  12, BENJAMIN MILLER.
    THOMAS ROSSITER JUNR.
    JOHN ARMET, proves to have taken the test of me in June, 1777.
  14, MATHIAS COPE, proves that he took of me the test in July 1777.
    JOHN GREBLE, of Philadelphia, Cooper, before Justice Young, in June 1777, took the test, since which he was constrained to swear allegiance to the Brittish, and now renews his former test.
  15, ANDREW HAMILTON.
    JACOB ZINCK, of Moyamensing, took the test of Benjamin Paschal in June 1777; was constrained to that of the Brittish, and now before me renounces the latter.

1778.

Sept. 17, BENJAMIN TOTTIE, proves that he in June 1777, took the test to the State before me. 2nd Certificate.

DAVID SALDRICH (his mark), not 18 years of age the 1st of June last.

18, PETER GRAB.

WILLIAM STOLL.

19, JAMES WEST.

JEROM INGIEZ, proves to have taken the State test in June 1777.

JOHN MATHES.

21, JOSEPH PALMER, proves his Attestation in June, 1777, before me.

24, TOBIAS RUDOLPH, proves his Attestation in Augt. 1777.

JACOB EHRENZELLER, proves his Attestation in June 1777.

25, CHRISTIAN RUDOLPH.

JAMES WALSH, proves his Attestation in June 1777.

26, SOLOMON HALLING, Second Surgeon in the General Military Hospitals.

THOMAS McDOWELL.

JOSEPH WOOD.

28, GEORGE HEYL, took the test of me the 25th day of June 1777; was constrained to swear allegiance to the Brittish, which he hath this day renounced.

WILLIAM ECKHART.

JOHN ORD ESQ., took the test July 10th 1777, & was constrained to swear allegiance to the Brittish, which he this day hath renounced.

1778.

Sept. 28, CHARLES PHILE, 1st Lt.

    JACOB LEHRÉ, proves to have Attested in June 1777.

    ROBERT FULLERTON.

29, ANDREW GEORGE (his mark).

    JAMES KINKEAD proves to have attested in Augt. 1777.

Oct. 2, WILLIAM MCCLATCHIE, proves to have attested before me in August 1777.

    CHARLES STEWART.

3, DANIEL GOSNER, proves to have attested in June 1777.

    JARED SAXTON.

    JOHN PORTER, late of Philada., proves to have taken the State test in June 1777. Affirmed. 2nd Certificate.

    JUSTINIAN FOX, proves to have taken the State test of me in June 1777. 2nd Certificate.

5, JAMES KELLEY, proves that at Carlisle, in February last, he took the Oath of Allegiance.

6, JOHN HELM, 1st Lieut. of 6th Penna. Regt., late a prisoner.

    JOHN GEORGE (his mark), Schuylkill.

    JOHN GEORGE JUNR. (his mark), Blockley.

    CHRISTIAN DISHONG.

9, EDMOND TOBIN.

    JOHN WHITE, proves to have taken the State test before me in June 1777.

10, DAVID SELLERS.

    CHRISTOPHER MIERS (his mark).

1778.

Oct. 12, JOHN LAWRENCE, Lieut., late prisoner of War.
    JOHN MORGAN, Lieut.,   do.   do.
    GEORGE GEORGE, proves to have taken the State test in Augt. 1777, before me.
    CHARLES GREER, a prisoner with the Enemy, while in the City.
    CHRISTIAN SLEIGH (his mark), proves to have taken the State Test in Augt. 1777.
    JOHN KERLIN JUNR., proves to have taken the State test in Augt. 1777.
    BENJAMIN SCULL, took the State test before me, the 2d day of Sept. 1777. No. 862.
    JOHN McKENNAN.
    JOHN STUART.
14, WILLIAM GLISSON.
    JOHN KOEHMLE, proves that he in June 1777, did take the Legal test before me.
    JOHN CALBANAN, proves that he was Qualified, before me, in June 1777.
    JOHN CLAZER (his mark), proves that he was Qualified before me in Sept. 1777.
    MICHAEL GITTS, proves that he was qualified before me in June 1777.
15, THOMAS BOOKER, proves that he was qualified in June 1777.
    PHILIP HOFFER,   do.   do.
    MATTHIAS WEISS,   do.   do.
16, THOMAS WADE (his mark).
    MICHAEL CANER, proves that he was qualified in July 1777, swore allegiance to the Brittish, and now renounces the same.

1778.

Oct. 17, THOMAS DICKSON, Cutter, renewed his certificate, 27th Augt. 1777. No. 849.

JOHN CROOK, proves that he was qualified in June 1777.

19, CHRISTIAN DAME, proves to have taken the test June 30th 1777.

JOHN FORSTER (his mark), Farmer.

C. MARTIN FORSTER (his mark).

ROBERT ROBSON (his mark), Mariner, a Brittish Prisoner.

DAVID TAGGART.

20, WILLIAM ARMSTRONG, of Philadelphia County, Major. Copy from Original June 30, 1777. No. 327.

21, JOHN RIDDLE, State Officer. Copy from Original June 30, 1777.

25, JOHN HIGNET KEELING.

JOHN CAMPBELL, proves taking the test in July 1777.

Nov. 2, WILLIAM WILSON.

CHARLES RITTER, proves to have taken the Oath before me in June 1777, was constrained to swear allegiance to the Brittish, which he hath now renounced.

ANDREW DOZ, late an Inhabitant of Jersey, where he took the Oath, as required by the law of that state.

MICHAEL GRATZ, late residing in Virginia, where he took the Oath to that state.

HEINRICH KIMHEL.

(53)

1778.

Nov. 7, JACOB MAUR, proves to have taken the test in June 1777.

WILLIAM STANLEY, schoolmaster, took the test in June 1777.

9, SHEWBART ARMITAGE.

10, PETER DE HAVEN, of Philada., Gentleman, produces his Certificate taken of me, 26th June 1777.

13, ISAAC HAYES, Blockley.

14, MICHAEL SCHMYSER, a prisoner lately exchanged.

16, SAMUEL HUMPHREYS, took the test in 1777.

17, JOHANN GEORGE DEGENHART, a Hessian Deserter.

18, RICHARD LUDGATE (his mark).

19, ALEXANDER TOD, took the Oath before me, June, 1777.

25, JOHN STONEMAN, Bensalem, took the test in 1777, of Col. Kirkbride. Sworn.

26, FREDERICK LINT, took the Oath in June 1777, was constrained to Brittish Allegiance, which he now hath renounced & renewed the former.

BENJAMIN CHAPMAN JUNR. Affirmed.

FRIEDERICH ERMANBERGER.

MARTIN PIERIE.

27, GEORGE STOUTE, Northern Liberties, took the test in June 1777.

JOHN LINNIBERGER (his mark).

HEINRICH KATZ, Whitemarsh.

28, GEORGE PEISS, Passiunk.

GODFREY SHISLER, do.

JOHN WHITE, do.

(54)

1778.

Nov. 30, MICHAEL SHIVER (his mark), proves to have taken the test of me, in June 1777.

    GEORGE SHAW, proves to have taken the test of me in 1777.

Dec. 2, WILLIAM GUINOP, proves to have taken the test before me in 1777.

    4, SAMUEL COUTTY, swears to have taken the test before me in the year 1777.

    5, FELIX LIBERSTIN.

    CASPER CLEIGNER (his mark).

    NICHOLAS QUEST (his mark).

    7, FREDERICK DUY.

    JOHN HIFFERNAN.

    JOHN WHITEMAN (his mark), late of Northern Liberties, Philada. County, proves by evidence, to have taken the Oath June 13th 1777.

    MORRIS WORREL, proves to have taken the Oath in June 1777.

    10, GEORG GEBHEART, swears to have taken the test in June 1777.

    JOSEPH LEWIS, on oath did take the test before me in July 1777.

    WILLIAM NICHOLAS (his mark), did take the test in June 1777.

    SAMUEL CRISPIN, on oath did take the test on or about June 1777.

    WILLIAM ASHTON, on oath did take the test on or about June 1777.

    JOHN FRALEY, on oath did take the test on or about June 1777.

According to the Act of 5th Decr. 1778.

1778.
Dec. 11, HEINRICH SCHWALLACH.

 PETER POWELL, on oath did take the test on or about June 1777, before me.

 EDWARD RIFFETS, on oath did take the test in June 1777 before me.

 18, MATHEW KNOX, Lieut., on oath proves that he was taken prisoner at fort Washington, exchanged the 22d September last, and returned to this State, the 24th of last month.

 WILLIAM CLARK, on Oath proves that he did take the Oath before me in 1777.

 DONALD MCINTOSH, foreigner, lately in the Brittish Service.

 JOHN EVERHART, on oath proves that in June 1777, he testified Allegiance before me.

1779.
Jan. 1, JOHANNES MÜLLER, a foreigner lately in the Brittish army.

 5, JOHN LINTON, in June 1777 did take the test before me.

 GEORGE SNYDER, on oath did take the Affirmation in 1777.

 8, PHILIP HEINRICHS, a foreigner lately in the Brittish service.

 11, ABRAHAM WAYNE, on oath proves that he did take & subscribe the test in 1777.

 22, DAVID EVERHARD, on oath proves that he did take and subscribe the test in June 1777.

1779.
Jan. 25, SAMUEL CHANNELL, on oath proves that he did take the test before me in June 1777.

27, ANDREW DAY, on oath proves that he did take the test oath before me in August 1777.

JEREMIAH WILLIAMS, on oath proves that he did take the test before me, in 1777.

Feb. 13, JACOB STETTENFIELD, a foreigner lately in the Brittish service.

CHRISTIAN OVERSTAKE (his mark), Northern Liberties, proves to have taken the test before me in 1777.

23, JAMES LIGHT, did take and subscribe the oath of allegiance before me the 3rd day of September 1777. Copy from Original.

25, JOHN MITCHEL, did take and subscribe the oath as by law directed in June 1777. 2d Certificate.

ANDREW ZEIGLER, of Swedesford did take the affirmation in June 1777.

March 16, JOHN FISHER, proves that he did take the test before me in 1777.

19, JOHN BARNHILL JUNR., not until now of the age of 18 years.

DAVID BEALER proves that he did take the test in the year 1777.

Apl. 2, WILLIAM LAWRENCE, on oath proves that he did take and subscribe as by law directed in 1777.

6, BENJAMIN MCVEAGH, by oath proves that he did take & subscribe as by law directed in 1777.

JOHN JACOB TRANSO, a German. A deserter from the Brittish.

1779.
Apl. 6, RICHARD TAYLOR, lately from Britain.
May 11, CHARLES BITTERS of Philada. late Breeches maker, made oath that he did take & subscribe before me in or about July 1777.

PHILIP STOCK, Gardner, on oath proves that he did take the test before me in June 1777.

17, THOMAS RICHMAN formerly a soldier in the Brittish Army. Deserted April 11, 1778.

GEORGE STOKES, on oath proves that he did take & subscribe in June 1777.

WILLIAM FECUNDAS, on Oath proves that he took & subscribed the oath in June 1777.

19, JEREMIAH QUIN, on Oath proves that he took & subscribed the Oath of Allegiance in June 1777.

20, MICHAEL GAMEBER, of Philada., Cooper, proves that he did take the test 27th June, 1777.

21, JOHANNES POTH, proves that he took the Oath required by law, the 22d day of July 1777.

ADAM POTH JUNR., proves that he took the Oath of Allegiance required, on the 22d day of July 1777.

WILLIAM HUNT, on Oath proves that about August in the year 1777, he did take & subscribe the oath according to law.

22, FRANTZ WILHELM HETTMANNKERGER, by evidence proves that he took & subscribed in July 1777.

JOHN HAIN, proves by evidence his taking before me in July 1777.

24, WILLIAM BROWN, of Philada., Tavern-Keeper, did in June 1777, take the test as appears by his Certificate. No. 447.

(58)

1779.

May 26, RICHARD SKELLORN, of Phila., Brass Founder, proves that he in 1777, before me took the Oath.

28, DANIEL SPENCER, proves that he in July 1777, did then take the test.

WILLIAM GOGGIN, Mariner, lately in the Brittish Service.

June 16, CORNELIUS COMEGYS JUNR., of Maryland, proves taking the test, according to law, in the year 1777.

JACOB BARGE, did affirm to the allegiance, according to law, in the year 1777.

17, ADAM LECHLER, proves that he did take the test, as by law directed in June 1777.

21, WILLIAM ALEXANDER, Son of Alexr. Alexander of this City, impressed by the Brittish in 1776, and in their service until June 1778.

26, WILLIAM WESTON, by evidence proves having taken the test in 1777.

July 30, PETER BAYNTON, testifies that he did take the test of Allegiance in 1777.

JAMES ROGERS, testifies that he took the test before me in 1777.

31, CASPER GOSNER, proves by Philip Wenemon his having taken the test before me in 1777.

CHRISTOPHER REED, proves by Capt. John Peters, that he took the test in the year 1777.

FRANCIS GUSSE, of Philada., Goldsmith, as appears by his certificate took the Oath of Allegiance, ye 28th day of June 1777. Was sworn by the Brittish.

(59)

1779.
July 31, GEORG BARDEEK, of Philada., Silversmith, proves by Francis Gusse, that he took the test ye 28th day of June 1777.

ROBERT FULLERTON, of Philada., Painter, proves by Capt. Joseph Wathens that he did take the test in the year 1777.

JOSEPH BOULTER, of Philada., Shoemaker, by Cadr. Dickinson, proves having taken the test before me in 1777.

CONRAD HANS, of Philada., Coachmaker, testifies having taken the test in the year 1777.

Aug. 2, CHRISTOPHER ADAMS, testifies that he took the test before me in the year 1777.

JOHN POLLARD, testifies that he did take the test before me, in the year 1777.

JOHN NICE, proves by Samuel Shrive that he took the test before Henry Chrest of Reading, the 21st day May 1778.

ALLAN MCCOLLIN, proves that he did take the test by Affirmation before me in the year 1777.

SAMUEL HONEYMAN, proves that he took the test in the year 1777.

JOSEPH ROBINETT, proves to have taken the test in 1777.

4, PETER GRANT, now of Philada., proves by Conrad Swetzer, that he in the year 1777 before Joshua Elder of Lancaster, did take the Oath of Allegiance.

JOHN ADAM KOEHLER, a deserter from the Brittish Army, now of Philada. Pewterer.

1779.

Aug. 4, GEORGE REINHART, proves to have taken the test, before me in the year 1777.

THOMAS DEAK, proves to have taken the test in 1777, before me.

8, JOHN HETHERINGTON, proves by Ludwick Shuder, that he took the test before Justice Moore, in the year 1777.

CHARLES LORDEN, of Philada., proves that he did take the test before me in 1777.

GEORGE HARLY, of Philada., Taylor, proves by Alexander Greenwood, that he took the test before me in the year 1777.

ALEXANDER GREENWOOD (his mark), of Philada., Shoemaker, proves by George Harley, that he took the test before me in the year 1777.

12, CONRAD ECKELMAN, proves by John Smith, that he, before me, in the year 1777, took the Oath.

BENEDICT SNEIDER, proves that he took the test before me in 1777.

JOHN SUTTON, proves that he took the test before me in the year 1777.

15, ALBRIGHT HAZLETON, proves that he took the test before me in the year 1777.

CASPER STULL, proves by Joseph Wathings that he took the test before me, in the year 1777.

ANDREW YOUNG, proves by certificate that he took the test with me in June 1777.

MATTIS POT, proves by Coron Kephard that he took the test before me in June 1777.

ABRAHAM ROBERTS, proves by Certificate that he took the test before me in June 1777. No. 476.

1779.

Aug. 15, CONRAD SCHIN, proves that he did take the test before me in the year 1777.

STEPHEN FOURAGE, proves that he took the test before me in 1777.

GEORGE RUTTER, proves that he took the test before me in the year 1777.

DANIEL CRAIG, of Philada., Hatter, proves that he took the test before me in the year 1777.

MICHAEL KRAFST, Tanner, proves by David Reshong that he did take the test before me in June 1777.

DAVID RESHONG, of Philada., Taylor, produces Certificate that he did take the test before me, June 30th 1777. No. 404.

JOSEPH OGDEN JUNR., proves that he took the test, the 1st day of July 1777, by Certificate produced.

EDWARD HUSTON, by Joseph Ogden Junr., proves that he took the Oath, the 1st day of July 1777.

19, CHARLES BLATZER. See the other record.

We the Subscribers do swear (or affirm) that I do renounce & refuse all allegiance to George the Third King of Great Britain, his heirs and successors; and that I will be faithful and bear true Allegiance to the Commonwealth of Pensilvania, as a free and Independent State; and that I will not at any time do or cause to be done any matter or thing that will be prejudicial or injurious to the freedom & Independence thereof as declared by Congress; and also that I will discover and make known to some one Justice of the said State, all treasons & traitorous conspiracies, which I now know, or hereafter shall know to be formed against this or any of the United States of America.

PLUNKET FLEESON.

Philadelphia, 1779.

1779.
- Aug. 14, LEWIS NICE, State Officer, proves that he in June 1777, before me did take the Oath of Allegiance as by law directed.
- 21, JACOB SMITH, late of this City, Harness-Maker, proves by James Gilingham, that he before me, in the year 1777, took the Oath of Allegiance as by law directed.
- 27, JOSHUA BURN, of Philada., Potter, proves by Original Certificate that the 1st day of July 1777, before me took the test of Allegiance according to Law. Original Certificate produced.

1779.

Sept. 1, CHRISTOPHER BURLY, proves that he in the Year 1777, before me took the Oath of Allegiance as by law directed.

ISRAEL MATTSON, of Philada., proves by James Lyons, that he before me did take the Oath as by law directed, in the year 1777.

2, ANDREW PARKHILL, proves by Daniel McCarey that he before me, took the Oath as by law directed, 30th June 1777.

DANIEL McCARY, of Philada., by Original Certificate proves that he took the Oath as by law directed before me the 30th June 1777.

27, THOMAS MESNARD, late a Brittish subject & lately from New-York.

30, JONATHAN STANTON, late in the Brittish service, now residing in this City. Breeches-Maker.

Oct. 11, JAMES GAMBLE, lately in the Brittish Sea service, as a Mariner.

WILLIAM VAUGHAN HITCHINGS, in the Brittish Mercht. Service, lately taken by an American Privateer.

12, DANIEL BARNHILL, lately returned from the Brittish fleet, into which he was pressed.

JOSEPH RUE, made proof that he took the test, the 1st day of July 1777. No. 665.

JACOB SCHRACK, proves by Edward Neffetts, that he took the test before me in June 1777.

THOMAS CHANNELL, took & subscribed the test before me, the 26th day of June 1777 as per Original Certificate.

1779.

Oct. 12, JOHAN CONRAD BECKMAN, late a soldier in the Hessian Army.

13, JACOB BOWER, late of Moyamensing, by testimony of Rudolph Feel, took and subscribed the Oath of Allegiance in June 1779.

14, SAMUEL SMITH; on affirmation proves that he took & subscribed the test of Allegiance in the year 1777.

20, JOSEPH BULKELEY, Mercht., lately arrived in this State from the Island of Eustatia.

WILLIAM SHIELL, M.D., lately arrived in this City from the City of Dublin.

Dec. 10, JOHAN PETER AHL, Taylor, a Hessian late in the Brittish Service.

CASPER LOVING, Taylor, a Hessian late in the Brittish Service.

PIERRE LEMAIGRE, a subject of France lately from that Kingdom, via N. York.

NICHOLAS PERREE, a native of France, lately from Guadelope.

22, JOHANN PANRERT, a Hessian late in the Brittish Service.

YORICK WUSMAN, a Hessian late in the Brittish Service.

27, JOSEPH OGDEN JUNR., proves by Original Certificate that he took & subscribed the test on affirmation, the 1st day of July 1777.

29, JOHANN XHART MELLOR, Baker, a Hessian from N. York, late in the Brittish service.

1780.

Jan. 4, JAMES LINCOLN, late from the City of Dublin.

1780.

Jan. 12, WILLIAM PRICHARD, lately from the Island of St. Eustatia.

Feb. 7, GEORGE MOORE, lately from the Massachusetts State where he took the Oath to the United States.

12, KERENCE DOWLING (his mark), late in the Hessian Army, deserted at the Battle of Monmouth, since a residenter in this State, by trade a woolcomber, & well recommended to me.

March 2, JAMES NUGENT, formerly a resident in the Jersey State, now of Philada.

April 8, JOHN SNELHART (his mark), a Hessian Deserter from the Brittish at N. York.

24, JOHN L. LEAR, Baker, a Hessian deserter from New York. Entered the American Service.

May 13, WILLIAM LINNARD, made Oath that he took the Oath of Allegiance, according to Law, in the month of June 1777, and hath lately lost his Certificate.

MARTIN CHRIST (his mark), deserted the Brittish Army, being an Anspacher & since the Army left this City.

16, PATRICK REILEY, Shoemaker, who says that he deserted the Brittish Service in 1778 & swore Allegiance to the States in that year, at Pitts Grove in this State & has lost his Certificate.

18, JOHN CONNOR, lately arrived from the Kingdom of Ireland. Mercht.

SIMÉON MEYLAND, a native of Switzerland, some time a resident in this City; by trade a Lapidary or Jeweller.

1780.

June 3, CARL LUDEWIG BARON V. BILOW, a Hessian, some time in the Brittish Service.

CHRISTIAN VON BECK, a Hessian, some time in the Brittish Service.

10, PHILIP BOUTMAN (his mark), of Southwark, by Thomas Booker proves that he took the test before in the year 1777.

WILLIAM PERKINS, late a Volunteer in Col. Mayland's Dragoons proves that he took the test about the month of Sept. in the year 1777. No. 900.

FRANCIS COLSON, House Carpenter, now a trader; lately arrived in this State from Hispaniola.

GEORG JOHNER, a Hessian, deserted from the Brittish Service in 1778.

12, ADAM SHETZLINE (his mark), has made proof by Godfred Gebler, that he took the test 29th June 1777.

GEORGE SPEEL, of Passiunk Township, made proof that he took the test before me in 1777.

CHRISTIAN LUTS, proves by John Young of Passiunk, that he did take the test in the year 1777.

DANIEL BARNS, of Philada., bricklayer proves from Original, that he took the test 1st day of July 1777.

DAVID NAER, of Philada., Nailor, proves by Godfrey Wetzel that he took the test 30th June, 1777.

14, JOHN HUGHES, Practitioner in Physick, lately arrived in this City from Hispaniola.

15, THOMAS SIMMONS, proves by Philip Boatman, that he took the test before me in 1777.

1780.

June 15, WILLIAM GRAY, of Philada., Brewer, proves by Original Certificate that he affirmed to the State test, the 26th June 1777.

27, THOMAS SMITH, a native of Bermuda, just arrived in this port from thence.

28, JAMES ALENBY, of Philada., Cooper proves by Rowland Pritchett, that he took the test before me in or about July 1777.

ROWLAND PRITCHETT, of Philada., Cooper, produces his Original Certificate No. 202 dated 28th June 1777.

30, WILLIAM BARBER, Captain, late a prisoner in Hispaniola; admitted to take the Oath of Allegiance (by order of Council).

July 11, JOHANNES SCHMITT, a Hessian, deserted from the Brittish in the year 1778, now married & settled in Springfield, Philada. Co.

20, JOHAN BARNARD SIMON, a Hessian, deserted from the Brittish army at New York, by trade a taylor, now married & settled in this City.

28, GEORGE KNOEPLER, a High German, deserted from the Brittish October 1779; recommended by John Jervis.

JOHN TELMAN, a German, deserted from the Brittish in October 1779, with a pass from the American Camp.

31, CHARLES TEIGH, a Hessian deserted from the Brittish in 1779, a hair dresser, married & settled in this City; asserted by John Wallace.

Aug. 3, PETER MALONE (his mark), formerly of Philada.,

1780.

breeches-maker, who hath lived in New York near five years & lately escaped to this City.

Aug. 4, NICHOLAS EGGERS, a Brittish Soldier, pressed in England, & deserted from Charlestown.

16, ABRAHAM FORST, Mercht., lately arrived in this City from Eustatia.

17, JOHN PATRICK LYNCH, Mercht., lately from the Kingdom of Ireland.

Sept. 22, WILLIAM DEWEES proves that he took the Oath of Allegiance in the year 1777 before me.

Oct. 4, MARCUS IOANE (his mark), Seaman, a Venitian by birth, arrived lately from Guadelope & has been some time in the Marine Service of this State.

10, JAMES SMITH, of the Forage Department, affirms that he took the test as by law directed in the year 1777, & had a certificate from me, which is lost.

JOSEPH NOURSE, of Philada., proved that he took & subscribed the Oath as by law directed in the year 1777.

Nov. 13, ALEXANDER BRODIE (his mark), Seaman, a native of Scotland lately arrived in this State from the Island Eustatia.

Dec. 13, HUMPHREY WILLIAMS, of Northern Liberties, Philada. Co., proves by Original Certificate, that he took & subscribed the Affirmation of Allegiance, the 1st of July 1777.

1781.

Jan. 11, GEORGE HOOK (his mark), born in Philada., a seaman having been some time a prisoner in New York, from whence he is lately discharged.

1781.
Jan. 27, MICHAEL CAIN (his mark), deserted from the Brittish Service in the year 1779. Labourer.
Feb. 3, THOMAS BECK (his mark), of Philada., shoemaker, proves that in the year 1777 before me he took and subscribed the Oath as by law directed.
March 1, CHRISTOPHER CLARK, Carpenter, lately arrived from a three years captivity in England, being a native of Boston.
 3, CONRAD KELLER, a Switzer, enlisted with the Brittish, deserted in Philada., & now following the trade of tinker.
 12, HEINRICH SCHMITT, a Hessian formerly in the Brittish Service, since in the American Artificers & discharged; by trade a Joyner.
 13, DANIEL BECKLEY, Carpenter, by Original Certificate No. 274, proves that he took the test to this State, according to the Act of 13th June 1777, the 30th day of the same month.
 JAMES BELL, of Philada., Carpenter, by Daniel Beckley proves that he took the test of the 13th of June 1777 before me, in July of the same year.
 31, ALEXANDER LOUIS O'NEILL, a native of France, late Captain in Genl. Count Pulaski's Legion.
April 19, ISAAC DAVIS, late of Harford Township, Chester County.
May 1, CHRISTOPHER FREDERICK DIEFFENBACH, by birth a German, arrived in this City about 18 months since; by trade a butcher.
 15, POWEL ADAM GARDENOK, a German Anspacher,

1781.

tinman & brazier, deserted from the Brittish near New York, about a year past.

May 28, JOHN MOYLAN, a native of Ireland, lately arrived in this City from the Camp of General Washington.

June 23, JOHN DAVID CRIMSHEW, Attorney at Law, late of New York.

25, JOHN PLEINY, a German by birth, lately arrived in this State and was a prisoner in England; taken on his way, being bound to Boston.

26, JOHANNES MARCUS (his mark), a native of Denmark, by trade an Instrument maker & turner; lately arrived in this state.

July 7, JAMES DAVIDSON, proves that about the month of June 1777, then being a professor in the College of Philada., he took the Oath of Allegiance & Fidelity as directed by law.

20, CHARLES ISAAC, arrived in the Brig Burton, from Charlestown. Mariner.

21, FREDERICK CHRISTIAN, of Philadelphia, Baker, by Bethenah Hodgkinson, proves that he in the year 1777, before me took & subscribed the Oath of Allegiance.

30, JOSEPH DOLBY, of Philada., Shoemaker, proves by Isabella Rogers that he in the year 1777 before me took & subscribed the Oath of Allegiance.

Aug. 28, HENRY HUDSON, late of Virginia. Wheelwright.

Oct. 1, JASPER ALEXANDER MOYLAN, late from the Kingdom of Spain. Student in Law.

9, JOSEPH GRAY, proves by William Gray that he took

1781.

& subscribed the Oath as directed by the Act of 1777 & had a Certificate, which is lost.

Nov. 5, WILLIAM AUSTIN SMITH.
ROBERT DOWNS, born in Philada.
BENJAMIN CARR.
CHARLES DECOSTER (his mark).
LEWIS DESANTEE (his mark).
BRYAN HYNES.
THOMAS MURPHY.
WILLIAM CODD (his mark).
} These 8 except Robert Downs are foreigners, Seamen, & now residenters in this State.

(JOHN GILCHRIST), a blackman. Deferred.

20, HENRY MEVINS, a soldier in the Brittish service, deserted about two years ago.

Dec. 26, JOHN GRIMES, formerly in the American Marines, taken prisoner by the Brittish & entered into that service; since taken by the Americans.

27, NICHOLAS ESLING, lately deserted from within the lines of the Brittish at New York.

1782.

Jan. 3, ANTONY MARSHAL, late a prisoner with the Brittish, a Seaman, native of Sicily, taken at Sea in an American Privateer.

16, SAMUEL MONTGOMERY BROWN, of the Kingdom of Ireland, lately arrived in this City from the Island of St. Thomas.

22, MARCUS MCCAUSLAND, of the Kingdom of Ireland, Mercht., lately arrived in this City from the Island of St. Thomas.

23, DANIEL ACKLEY, by trade a Carpenter, a native & inhabitant of N. York, deserted from thence and lately come to this City.

1782.

Jan. 23, THOMAS PETTIT, a native of New York & an inhabitant, deserted from thence & lately arrived in this City; by trade a Silver Smith.

30, GEORG HUBER, an Anspacher, in the Brittish Service, deserted in the year 1778, when in this City & hath continued in this state ever since; by trade a taylor.

Feb. 12, WILLIAM WILSON, formerly in the American Army in Canada, taken by the enemy, escaped from them and brought prisoner to this City & discharged by the Board of War; by trade a hatter.

JACOB CALB (his mark).
JOHANNES MAYER (his mark).
} Deserters from the Anspach troops, before the surrender of the Brittish Army in Virginia.

21, BENJAMIN JAMES MARCER, formerly a resident of this State, lately from New York; by trade a Shoemaker.

22, GEORGE LARRISON of Cohansey in the State of New Jersey; turner.

JAMES COLLINS, Mercht., late of the Kingdom of Ireland, & lately come to this City from New York.

ALEXANDER SEMPLE, lately arrived in this City from Jamaica by way of New York. Mercht.

March 13, WILLIAM ATCHISON, Mariner, a native of Scotland, from the Island of St. Thomas.

April 2, CHARLES STILWIL, a native of New York, lately from Bermuda.

1782.

April 2, JOHN HAMILTON, a sea-faring man, born in Ireland; last from Bermuda.

4, JAMES GENTLE, now of Philada., Bookbinder, was a prisoner in England & beyond the sea until within about a year last past.

THOMAS NEWARK, late an Inhabitant of Salem Co., now of the City of Philada. Taverner.

HENRY SPARKS, late of Salem County, now an Inhabitant in Philada. City Corder.

5, NICHOLAS KIRWAN, formerly an inhabitant of Antigua, lately of the City of Philada.

NICHOLAS DEERING, formerly an inhabitant of Antigua, lately of Philada. Mercht.

10, CORNELIUS BARNS (his mark). } Three soldiers deserted the Brittish Army, now on the Staten Island, examined by Council and admitted.
RICHARD PERRY (his mark). alias Tempest.
JAMES HURST (his mark).

15, GEORGE OLIVER, a Seaman taken prisoner into New York, late a pilot of the river Delaware, deserted the Brittish Service at Charlestown and arrived in Philada. in September last.

17, JOHN HERBERT GRUBB. } Deserters from the Brittish Army at N. York recommended by Secty Matlack.
ISAAC KING (his mark).
JOSEPH MAYNARD.

May 4, JOHN HENRY, formerly of Philada., taken prisoner in the Brittish Service in South Carolina.

(74)

1782.

May 8, LUKE THOMAS, formerly of Philada., latterly of New York; returned by permission from the Council of this State.

9, DANIEL MONTGOMERY, Taylor, deserted from the Brittish Army in Philada. in 1777.

GEORGE HINTON, born in Philada., apprentice to John Fox, taken away with the Brittish, taken prisoner and now discharged.

13, GEORGE INGLIS, lately from Jamaica by way of New York.

15, PATRICK LANDERKEN (his mark), formerly in the Brittish Mercht. Service; by trade a Cooper.

June 7, CORNELIUS DEY, a seaman deserted from the Brittish Service.

JEREMIAH MURRY (his mark), a seaman deserted from the Brittish Service.

11, JOHANN ROTHMANN, deserted from the Brittish Infantry in the year 1778.

12, ROBERT MCCAUSLAND, lately from Antigua, by way of New York. Mercht.

20, WILLIAM MONTGOMERY BROWN, Mercht. from Ireland to New York, and to Philada. with a flag.

July 2, WILLIAM PETERS JUNR., of this City, taken prisoner by the Brittish in the year 1777; taken at sea.

(CAPT. JOHN MCNACHTANE) took and subscribed the Oath of Allegiance the 30th day of June 1777, as appears by Original Certificate. No. 330.

10, JAMES STEEL, formerly in the Brittish Service taken at Yorktown & discharged; by trade a Sadler.

1782.

July 10, JOHN KENEDY. ⎫ Deserters from the Brittish,
JOHN FITZPATRICK ⎬ permitted by Council to con-
(his mark). ⎭ tinue in this State. Labourers.

PATRICK O'DONNELL, lately from New York & permitted by the president.

16, SILVESTER WHITE (his mark), lately deserted from the Brittish on York Island; permitted by the Presdt.

29, JOHN KEYSER, deserted from the Brittish Army & Hessian line 4 years past.

Aug. 3, WILLIAM BLAKE, an inhabitant of Boston, on his way to Newburyport, express for Donaldson & Co.

TIMOTHY HICKEY, says he deserted the Brittish Service about four years ago.

5, JOHN WRIGHT, deserted from the enemy about three years ago; by trade a Hoosier.

JAMES STOKES, deserted from the enemy, hath re-sided in this City above two years; a dealer in goods.

SAMUEL READ (his mark), deserted from the Brittish about eighteen months since; a wool card maker.

ABRAHAM KING (his mark), deserted from the enemy & hath resided in Philada. four years; wool comber.

JOHN MOORE, deserted from the enemy about a year & followed his trade of Taylor in Philada.

CHRISTIAN BUSH (his mark), deserted from the enemy about 4 years. Cheap fitter in Philada.

1782.

Aug. 5, CHARLES DANIEL BOOS, deserted from the enemy about 4 years and kept store in Philada. the last year.

GEORGE HERFFORD, deserted about nine months from the Brittish Service; by trade a Silversmith.

JOHANNES LOOMSBACH, deserted above two years from the Brittish Service and hath resided that time in Philada. Hostler.

MARTIN CHRIST (his mark), deserted the Brittish Service above four years; by trade a Hozier.

6, JOHN BROWN, deserted the Brittish Service about 4 years ago from the Hessian line.

CHARLEAS HEATLY, lately from St. Christophers; Barrister at Law.

PETER KEMBLE, from St. Christophers, Mercht.

HUGH MOORE, from St. Christophers, Mercht.

JACOB JARVIS, from Antigua, Mercht.

THOMAS MCCLENNEY, from Antigua, Mariner.

GEORGE READ, from Antigua, Clark.

CONRAD HANKEL, late in the Brittish Service, a waggoner & came to this City, about 4 years ago.

FRANCIS KREANING, deserted the Brittish Service & Hessian Line at the Battle of Monmouth; Shoemaker.

JOHN SHEE, deserted above three years from the Brittish Service; hair dresser.

HENRY DEWERS, deserted the Brittish Service above three years; shoemaker.

VALENTIN SCHMITT, deserted the British Service about four years; a barber.

1782.

Aug. 6, FRANCIS OTTO, deserted the Brittish Service about 4 years, a Hessian; by trade a book-binder.

JOHANNES PARKMANN, deserted the Brittish Service & Hessian Line about one year; by trade a tanner & currier.

JOHANN BISHOP, deserted the Brittish Service & Hessian Line about one year; by trade a Shoe maker.

GEORGE TODD, deserted the Brittish Service in 1777, by trade a Barber.

FERGUS McCREA (his mark), deserted the Brittish Service about two years. Labourer.

JAMES McMILLEN (his mark), deserted the Brittish Service near 4 years; by trade a Mason.

PETER BRUCE (his mark), deserted the Brittish Sea Service about six weeks; seaman.

ADAM OPPERMAN, deserted the enemy & Hessian line about 4 years; by trade a Weaver.

JAMES RONALS, deserted the enemy about 2 years past; labourer.

FRANCIS REYNHART (his mark), a Hessian deserter from Virginia; labourer.

WILLIAM GARMAN (his mark), a Hessian deserter from New York; Labourer.

7, CASPAR GOLDSCHMITT, a Hessian deserter from New York about 4 years past; schoolmaster.

ADAM CULLMAN, a Hessian deserter from New York lately; Shoemaker.

JOHAN MICHAEL AIRHOTT, deserted the Brittish & line of Anspach 2 years past.

1782.

Aug. 7, FREDERICK GRUNWOLD, deserted the Brittish & Hessian Line from Virginia above one year; a Baker.

HENRY BLATTERMAN, deserted the Brittish and Hessian Line about 3 years from New York; a Baker.

PHILIP SMITH.

JOHN DURIE (his mark), deserted the Brittish & Hessian Line above 3 years; Labourer.

DANIEL BENDER (his mark), deserted the Brittish & Hessian Line above 4 years past; labourer.

KENETH MCLEAN, a Scotchman, deserted the Brittish at the Battle of Monmouth; labourer.

JOHN REYNARD (his mark), deserted the Brittish from Virginia about two years; Labourer.

RICHARD MCGREGOR (his mark), a Scotchman, deserted the Brittish at Stony Point in 1779.

ARTHUR BARNS (his mark), an Irishman, deserted the Brittish at Camden in Carolina in 1780.

JOHN MARTIN ZIPOLT, deserted the Brittish & Hessian Line at the Battle of Monmouth; Barber.

GEORGE KEIDEL (his mark), deserted the Brittish on Long Island in April last; Baker.

PETER DAVIS (his mark), deserted the Brittish Army and Hessian line at Kingsbridge last month.

WALDROP SIEMAN, deserted the Brittish Army & Hessian line at Kingsbridge, 4 years past. Wheelwright.

GODFRIED WASPHAL, deserted the Brittish at Gloster, a Hessian; Hozier.

1782.

Aug. 7, JACOB RANGANER (his mark), an Anspacher deserted the Brittish at Kingsbridge near 3 years; Taylor.

JOHN LEWIS (his mark), deserted the Brittish at Kingsbridge, February last, a Hessian; labourer.

BERNHARD KOEHLER, a Hessian, deserted the Infamous Arnold last year; loom weaver.

ANTHONY GEORGE, deserted the Brittish Army & Line of Waldeckers about 4 years past; a pedler.

WILLIAM KOY (his mark), deserted the Brittish Army in Virginia about one year past; labourer.

TIMOTHY RUSSEGUE, an American, deserted the Brittish at Gloster in Virginia in 1781; labourer.

JAMES JACKSON, deserted the Brittish Army at Gloster in Virginia in 1781; labourer.

8, JAMES BOYLE (his mark), deserted the Brittish Army in 1778, a Scotchman; by trade a Weaver.

JOHN MCGREGOR (his mark), an Irishman, deserted the Brittish Army at Kingsbridge in 1778; labourer.

MICHAEL GEHRING, deserted the Brittish Army last fall from Canada; labourer.

DANIEL VOGEL, deserted the Brittish Army at St. Johns in Canada about a year past; labourer.

GEORG BRUNER, deserted the Brittish Service & Line of Anspach last fall; taylor.

JOHAN HARTLAN, deserted the Brittish Army & Line of Anspach from Virginia last fall; brewer.

JOHAN KLEIN, deserted the Brittish Service & Line of Anspach from Virginia last fall; blacksmith.

1782.

Aug. 8, JOHN ROBERT (his mark), deserted the Brittish Service & Hessian Line; labourer.

JAMES MCMULLEN, deserted the Brittish Army from York near 3 years past; labourer.

LEWIS ILGEN, deserted the Brittish Service & Line of Anspach from Kingsbridge; labourer.

WILLIAM ESENBECK, lately deserted the Brittish Service and Line of Anspach; labourer.

GOTFRED SOYTDER, deserted the Brittish Service & Hessian Line three years past; wheelwright.

BALTUS SCHUNEL, deserted the Brittish Service & Line of Anspach in 1778 from Rodessland; House carpenter.

9, GODFREY ROSENBERGER (his mark), deserted the Brittish & Line of Hessians at Kingsbridge about a year past; butcher.

JOHANN SCHEILER, deserted the Brittish at Fort Ann & the Hessian Line at Fort Ann above five years past; labourer.

PETER LEECH (his mark), deserted the Brittish Army from Jersey in 1778; labourer.

AUGUSTUS KAJE, deserted the Brittish Service & Hessian Line above two years past; Shoemaker.

LUDWIG MEAYN, deserted the Brittish Service & Hessian Line from Jersey last year; wheelwright.

FRIEDERICH MIDDLEHAUSER, deserted the enemy & Hessian Line at Kingsbridge in Nov. 1779; Skindresser.

EDWARD RYAN, deserted the Brittish Army at Monmouth in 1778; hairdresser.

1782.
Aug. 9, CHRISTIAN MULLER, deserted the Brittish Service & Hessian Line in Virginia in 1781; Gardener.

GEORGE ESHRICK (his mark), deserted the Brittish Service and Line of Anspach in Virginia this year; gardener.

GEORGE STEAR, deserted the Brittish Service & Hessian Line at New York above two years past; a baker.

WILLIAM MCDONALD, deserted the Brittish Army at New York in Decr. 1781; Taylor.

10, CHRISTIAN KAUCH, deserted the Brittish Service, a Brunswicker, in the year 1781; labourer.

CHRISTOPHER ARMSTRONG, deserted the Brittish Army at Monmouth in the year 1778; labourer.

FRANCIS REED (his mark), deserted the Brittish Army at Virginia, May 17th 1782; labourer.

HEINRICH WIEST, deserted from the Brittish Service & Hessian Line at Germantown in 1777; Shoemaker.

CHRISTIAN FRIEDERICH REINBOTT, deserted the Brittish Service & Hessian Line at Kingsbridge in February 1782; Shoemaker.

GEORG ADAM ALBERT, deserted the Brittish Service & Hessian Line from Virginia last year; Locksmith.

ANTHONY POWELL, deserted the Brittish Service & Hessian Line at Kingsbridge in 1781; Sadler.

RICHARD MANDRY, deserted the Brittish Army in North Carolina in 1781; Shoemaker.

1782.

Aug. 10, WILLIAM HOOK (his mark), deserted the Brittish Army in the Jersey State 1778; Weaver.

CHARLES HAZLEY, deserted the Brittish Army in Virginia, August 1781; Labourer.

HEYNRICH HEYNEMAN, deserted the Brittish Service & Line of Anspach at York, Virginia in 1781; Potter.

BALTHAZER DILL, deserted the Brittish Service & Line of Hessians at Brandywine in 1777; Blacksmith.

JOHANN VALTIN EDELING, deserted the Brittish Service & Line of Hessians at Kings Bridge in the year 1781. Wheelmaker.

12, LEWIS PRICE (his mark), deserted the Brittish Service & Hessian Line in Jersey 1778. Labourer.

THOMAS WILLIAMS, deserted the Brittish Army in North Carolina in 1781. Shoemaker.

VALENTIN BUCHHOLTZ deserted the Brittish Service & Line of Hessians at New York about two months past. Miller.

JAMES DUNBAR (his mark), Deserted the Brittish Army in Jersey in 1778. Labourer.

LUDWIG DUDENGÖSS, deserted the Brittish Service & Hessian Line at Kingsbridge in 1781. Labourer.

HENRY HEIZER (his mark), deserted the Brittish Service & Hessian Line, at Charles Town in 1781. Labourer.

PHILIP KÖHR, deserted the Brittish Service & Hessian Line at Benington in 1778. Skindresser.

1782.
Aug. 12, LAWRENCE EDDLESTON, Deserted the Brittish Sea Service from the Renown in 1779. Cheesemaker.

GOTTLIEB ANTON, deserted the Brittish Service & Hessian Line at Stony Point in 1779. Labourer.

GEORG RUMEL deserted the Brittish Service & Line of Anspach at Rhode Island in 1778.

THOMAS HINES (his mark), deserted the Brittish Army in Connecticut about three years past. Labourer.

CASPAR MILLER, deserted the Brittish Service in Virginia about one year, a Hessian; by trade a Weaver.

JOHANNES GIESSLER, deserted the Brittish Service & Hessian Line at New York March last. Weaver.

JOHN KNOWLES (his mark), deserted the Brittish Army at Virginia in 1781. Labourer.

MICHAEL DALLER, deserted the Brittish Army & Hessian Line at Germantown in 1778. Taylor.

JOHANNES OTTO, deserted the Brittish Service & Hessian Line in South Carolina in 1781. Weaver.

JOHN MUSTER, deserted the Brittish Service & Hessian Line at Staten Island about 3 years past. Weaver.

JOHANN LUTZ, deserted the Brittish Service & Line of Anspach at Virginia in 1781. Baker.

ANDREAS KIPP, deserted the Brittish Service & Hessian Line at New York about 2 months past. Weaver.

JOHANN GLICK, deserted the Brittish Service & Hessian Line at New York last month. Labourer.

1782.

Aug. 12, JOHN RICHHOWSER (his mark), deserted the Brittish Army in Virginia Septr. last. Tanner.

ERNST ENDESRUGGERN, deserted the Brittish Service & Hessian Line at Long Island three months past. Shoemaker.

CHRISTOPHER TILMAN (his mark), deserted the Brittish Service & Hessian Line at N. York three years past. Cutler.

HANCE KILLAMER (his mark), deserted the Brittish Service & Hessian Line at Kingsbridge last fall. Labourer.

HENRY MYERS, late Surgeon's Mate, deserted in May last from Long Island.

13, VANDEL STOUP (his mark), deserted the Brittish Service & Hessian Line at Kingsbridge, January 1781. Labourer.

JACOB FRANCIS, deserted the Brittish Army at Monmouth in 1778. Mason.

ROBERT MELVIN (his mark), deserted the Brittish Army at Charlestown in 1781. Labourer.

GEORGE WALKER, deserted the Brittish Army at Kingsbridge in 1779. Labourer.

JOHANN HEINRICH WAHL, deserted the Brittish Service at Kingsbridge in 1781. Shoemaker.

14, CHRISTIAN KEAVORT (his mark), deserted the Brittish Service & Hessian Line at Carolina Febr. 1782. Weaver.

GEORGE ANDERSON (his mark), deserted the Brittish Army at Virginia in 1781. Labourer.

JOHN MILLER (his mark), deserted the Brittish & Hessian Line in Philada. 1778. Labourer.

1782.

Aug. 14, JOHN SEMPLE (his mark), deserted the Brittish Service in England, came to America & served one year in the American Army. Labourer.

PETER FRANSES, deserted the Brittish Service & Hessian Line at N. York in June last. Barber.

GEORGE BURNHOUSE (his mark), deserted the Brittish & Hessian Line in 1781. Carpenter.

JOHN SPALTER (his mark), deserted the Brittish Service & Hessian Line in Jersey 1778. Labourer.

WILLIAM BERRY, deserted the Brittish Army at Statten Island in 1778. Labourer.

JOHN ATKINSON, deserted the Brittish Sea Service & Ship Hussar at New York in 1779.

FELIX PLAIN, deserted the Brittish Service at Georgia in 1781. Baker.

HEINRICH ALBERT, deserted the Brittish & Line of Anspach in Virginia in 1781. Taylor.

HENRY DEMD (his mark), deserted the Brittish & Hessian Line in Jersey in 1778. Labourer.

ZACARIAS PITTMAN (his mark), deserted the Brittish & Hessian Line at Jersey in 1778. Taylor.

THOMAS JACKSON (his mark), deserted the Brittish Army at New York in 1778. Brass founder.

JOSEPH WHITE deserted the Brittish Army at N. York 1778. Labourer.

HENRY HARRIS (his mark), deserted the Brittish Army at New York in July last. Labourer.

PETER SHUCHARD, deserted the Brittish Army & Hessian Line at N. York in 1779. Schoolmaster.

1782.

Aug. 14, MARTIN CASPER, deserted the Brittish Army & Hessian Line in 1778. Baker.

GUSTAV CLARCK, deserted the Brittish Service & Line of Anspach in Virga. in 1781. Labourer.

JOHN RUNDLEMAN (his mark), deserted the Brittish Army & Hessian Line at New London in 1777. Rope Maker.

JOHN HARPER (his mark), deserted the Brittish Army at New York in 1780. Labourer.

15, JOHN ALBERT SHOVE (his mark), deserted the Brittish Service & Hessian Line in Jersey 1778. Labourer.

WILLIAM SHELVOUGH (his mark), deserted the Brittish Army at Virginia in 1781. Labourer.

FRIEDERICH SHUMAN, deserted the Brittish Army in Philada. in 1778. Labourer.

JOHANN HEINRICH FRICHMAN, deserted the Brittish Service & Hessian Line in Jersey in 1778. Labourer.

WILLIAM CONNELL, deserted the Brittish Sea Service from the Hunter Sloop at Sandy Hook in 1779. Weaver.

JAMES ROBINSON, deserted the Brittish Army in Jersey in 1778. Weaver.

JOHN BLAIN (his mark), deserted the Brittish Army in Philada. 1778. Labourer.

16, JACOB SHREIBER, deserted the Brittish Service & Hessian Line in Jersey in 1778. Labourer.

WILHELM CASSELLMAN, deserted the Brittish Service & Hessian Line in Jersey in 1780. Labourer.

1782.

Aug. 15, JOSEPH CROOK (his mark), deserted the Brittish Army at Kingsbridge in 1780. Weaver.

THOMAS HOOKER (his mark), who deserted the Brittish Army at Monmouth in 1778. Baker.

MATTHIAS EIKHART (his mark), deserted the Brittish Service & Hessian Line at White Plains in 1778. Taylor.

BERNHARD SHAGERT, deserted the Brittish Service & Hessian Line at Philada. in 1778. Taylor.

FRIEDERICH BLOSS, who deserted the Hessian Line in Virginia in 1781. Taylor.

17, CONRAD LEITSHOK, deserted the Brittish Service & Hessian Line in March last from N. York. Weaver.

JOHANNES SAUTTER, deserted the Brittish Service & Hessian Line at Kingsbridge in July last. Baker.

GEORGE VENSELL (his mark), deserted the Brittish Service & Hessian Line at Kingsbridge in 1779. Taylor.

GEORGE STEPHNON (his mark), deserted the Brittish Service & Hessian Line in Jersey in 1778. Labourer.

JONAS HAVESSTRICK (his mark), deserted the Brittish Service & Hessian Line at Philadelphia in 1778. Labourer.

CONRAD GOTLIB (his mark), deserted the Brittish Army at the head of the Elk in 1777. Labourer.

TICTUS HUNTHEIMER (his mark), deserted the Brittish Service & Line of Anspach in Virginia 1781. Rope Maker.

1782.

Aug. 19, FREDERICK DEIMLING, deserted the Brittish Service & Hessian Line at Charlestown S. C. in 1780. Organ Builder.

THOMAS SAMPLE, a Lieut., formerly in the Brittish Service, from which he was discharged in Philadelphia in 1777. Mariner.

JOHN DOUGLASS (his mark), deserted the Brittish Army in Philada. in 1777. Labourer.

JOHN ASSMUS, deserted the Brittish Army in Jersey in 1778. Locksmith.

MICHAEL MCMAHON, deserted the Brittish Horse at Kingsbridge in 1779. Hairdresser.

MAURICE BARNS, deserted the Brittish Army in S. Carolina in 1780. Taylor.

SAMUEL CASEY (his mark), deserted the Brittish Army in S. Car. in 1781. Labourer.

ROBERT TIVIMAN, deserted the Brittish Army from Paulus Hook in 1780. Shoemaker.

JAMES BOYL, who deserted the Brittish Army at Dobbs' Ferry last month. Seaman.

FRIEDERICH KORLODER, who deserted the Brittish Service and Hessian Line last winter.

JOHN HAMILTON, deserted the Brittish Army & train of Artillery at Monmouth in 1778. Minor.

ABRAHAM JAGGER, deserted the Brittish Army in Jersey in 1778. Weaver.

JOHN COVE, deserted the Brittish Army on the Sarcy in 1778. Smith.

HEINRICH PRESUHN, deserted the Brittish Service & Hessian Line at Monmouth in 1778. Shoemaker.

1782.
Aug. 21, JOSHUA KELSEY, deserted the Brittish Army at Stony Point in 1779. Shoemaker.
JOHANN NIEMOND, deserted the Brittish Service & Hessian Line in Virginia 1781. Baker.
MARKS MCCARTY, deserted the Brittish Army at Long Island in the year 1782. Carrier.
JONATHAN CARLIN, deserted the Brittish Army & train of Artilery at Kingsbridge in 1779. Hozier.
GEORGE DERRY (his mark), deserted the Brittish Service & Hessian Line at Paulus Hook the 30th of last month. Labourer.
22, MATTHEW BALAM, took the Oath Decemr. 1778.
JOHN MAY, deserted the Brittish Army at Long Island in May last. Turner.
GEORGE HUGGINS, deserted the Brittish Sea Service from New York in April last. House Carpenter.
23, JOHN RITGIE, deserted the Brittish Service & Hessian Line in Jersey 1778. Carpenter.
24, DANIEL SINKET, deserted the Brittish Army in Jersey in 1778. Labourer.
26, BENJAMIN DOW, deserted from New York 18th inst. Blacksmith.
DAVID HOWELL (his mark), deserted from New York 18th Inst. Blacksmith.
27, THOMAS COX, Escaped from N. York the 18th Inst. Blacksmith.
JOHN MIDWINTER, Escaped from New York the 18th Inst. Blacksmith.
28, JOHN SPOONER, who deserted the Brittish Army at N. York the 15th Inst. Labourer.

1782.

Aug. 28, JACOB ZIMMERMAN, deserted the Brittish Service and Hessian Line in Virginia 1781. Weaver.

29, ADAM FRITENHEILER, deserted the Brittish Service & Hessian line in Virginia in Septr. last. Baker.

30, HENRY QUEERFORT, deserted Burgoyne's Army & Hessian Line in 1778. Carpenter.

JAMES BRUNTON, taken prisoner in the Brittish Service in Jersey in 1781. Surgeon.

31, PETER BLEIJER, deserted the Brittish Service & Hessian Line in Virginia Octr. 1781. Butcher.

PETER KEMMEL (his mark), deserted the Brittish Service & Hessian Line at N. York July 1782. Labourer.

Sept. 3, VALENTINE BORNMAN, deserted the Enemy & Hessian Line at Monmouth in 1778. Labourer.

5, WILLIAM ROBERTS (his mark), deserted the Brittish Army in Philadelphia June 1778. Labourer.

JAMES WIEAR, says he was prisoner with the Enemy 3 years & escaped from N. York 2 Inst. Taylor.

7, GEORGE BUCH JONES (his mark), says he deserted the Enemy at Canada from Carlton's Army in 1777. Carpenter.

FERDINAND WAGNER, says he deserted the Enemy in S. Carolina in 1781. Schoolmaster.

GILBERT HUNT (his mark), says he deserted the Enemy in Virginia, Inlisted in Maryland & is discharged. Labourer.

CONROD DEAN (his mark), says he deserted the Hessian Line at Fort Washington in 1771. Labourer.

1782.

Sept. 11, MATTHIAS HOHNERSN, deserted the Enemy & Hessian Line in Georgia in March last. Comb Maker.

WILLIAM THOMAS (his mark), deserted the Brittish Army at Staten Island 8th Inst. Nailer.

12, HENRY OSMOS (his mark), says he deserted the Brittish Army at Billingsport in 1777, a Hannoverian.

13, SAMUEL SUMMERS, deserted the Brittish Army in Connecticut in 1779.

23, KENNETH CAMPBELL, THOMAS BATLEY (his mark), } deserted from the Enemy at Staten Island & from the 22nd Regt. Labourers.

24, WILLIAM SMITH, deserted the Brittish Line from Staten Island 17th Inst.

25, MATTHEW COULTHURST, lately arrived in this City from Nantz. Attorney at Law.

JAMES BOWEN, an Inhabitant of N. Y. lately made his escape from thence. Joyner.

FREDERIC GRANER, deserted the Enemy & Line of Anspach at York Island 15th Inst.

JOHANN FRIEDELBACH, deserted the Enemy & Line of Anspach at York Island 15th Inst.

Oct. 3, PHILIP LYON, Ship Captain belonging to Philadelphia.

7, WILLIAM MACPHERSON, Major in the American Army since Sept. 1779.

8, JOSEPH ALSTON, a Native of Philada. in Martina, on publick Service from 1776 to 1781.

WILLIAM HUCKEL, deserted the Brittish Service in Philada. in the year 1778. Upholsterer.

1782.
Oct. 8, JOHN DUGUID JUNR., an Officer in the Pena. Line in 1776, taken prisoner at fort Washington.

KENNEDY MCFARLAND, deserted the Brittish Service in Novemr. last.

GEORGE EDDY, lately arrived to the age of eighteen. Affirmed.

10, DANIEL BOLAND (his mark), deserted the Brittish at the White Plains in 1776, served in the American Navy & lately discharged.

14, DAVID DENNY, Midshipman on board the Mede Frigate New York 1st Octor. Inst.

19, WILLIAM WILLSON, deserted the Brittish Service into which he was prest when prisoner at New-York as he says.

WILLIAM DOWNEY (his mark), a prisoner at New York, pressed from the prison ship & deserted.

Nov. 2, JOHAN SCHNEIDER deserted the Brittish & Hessian Line near Kingsbridge in 1777. Surgeon's Mate.

5, HENRY HAMMER, deserted the Brittish Service & Hessian Line at Paulus Hook 1st Inst. Weaver.

HENRY OILL, deserted the Enemy from York Island the 1st Inst. Taylor.

FRIEDERICH SHMID, a prisoner of War, discharged by the Council of State.

10, CONROD LUTHER (his mark), deserted the Enemy & Hessian Line in Jersey in 1778.

13, JOHN ANDREW LUZER (his mark), deserted the Enemy & Hessian Line at Paulus Hook 2d Inst. Labourer.

CARL BEYER, who deserted the Enemy. Surgeon's

1782.

Mate in the Hessian Line 3 years past, now married & settled in Northampton.

Nov. 21, NICHOLAS DOWNING, a seaman from Maryland on his way to Rhode Island to which he belongs.

DANIEL PLATT, lately from Maryland on his way to Connecticut to which he belongs.

22, JOSEPH BIDGOOD, lately arrived from Charlestown. Dealer.

23, JOHN MCGOUEN (his mark), who deserted the Enemy at Staten Island in Octr. last. Labourer.

25, ALEXANDER MURPHY (his mark), late Corporal in the 40 Brittish Regiment, deserted at Staten Island 20th Inst. Labourer.

JOHN BURRAGE (his mark), late Corpl. in above regt., deserted same time. Weaver.

27, JAMES DAVIS, who deserted the Brittish Service at the head of the Elk in 1777. Labourer.

HENRY GRANT (his mark), says he deserted the Enemy & Hessian Line at York Island 19th Inst. Dyer.

30, ROBERT STEWART, Mercht., lately from Ireland.

JOHN MILLER, who deserted the Brittish Service & Hessian Line in Jersey 1778. Weaver.

Dec. 2, ROBERT SIM, who deserted the Brittish Army at New York the 13th Inst.

3, JOHN CULNAN, from the Kingdom of Ireland, Resident in America about two years.

5, JOHN BLACK, formerly in the Waggon Department of this State.

1782.

Dec. 5, WILLIAM KELLY, well recommended from State of New Hampshire.

7, ANDREW COWIE, a prisoner taken by the Brittish at Pensacola. Escaped from N. York.

FRANCIS MOUSSU DELONGUAY, native of France lately arrived in this City. Mercht.

JOHN COFFMAN, from Maryland with a pass, by trade a tanner & currier.

11, CHARLES RINALDI, from Boston with a pass, on his way to Baltimore on Station.

JOHN LAYCOCK, a Frenchman with a pass, from Boston on his way to Baltimore.

14, HENRY HAMILTON, lately arrived in this City from St. Kitts Via Edentown, N. Carolina. Mercht.

16, JOHN MEARS (his mark), deserted the Enemy in S. Carolina in 1780. Labourer.

17, CASPAR SCHMIDT, appears to have deserted the Enemy & Hessian Line at York Island in 1779.

18, WILHELM SITZDORFF, of the 60th Brittish Regt., deserted at Long Island in October last.

JOMEL MENTZ (his mark), of the 60th Regt., deserted at Long Island in October last.

23, WILLIAM SCOTT, taken prisoner by the Brittish at Pensacola, escaped from N. Y. 19th Novr. last.

26, JOHN SHIELDS, deserted the Enemy from on board the Lion Man of War at N. York 29th Novr. last.

1783.

Jan. 30, PAUL WEAVER, who deserted the Enemy & Hessian Line at Charlestown in 1780.

(95)

1783.
Jan. 31, SAMUEL FRASER, deserted the Brittish Army at New York the 25th Inst. Labourer.

DANIEL MCCARTER (his mark), deserted the Brittish Army at New York 25th Inst.

Feb. 6, JAMES ANDERSON, deserted the Brittish from the lines of New York in 1779. Labourer.

17, HENRY MILLER, a Hessian prisoner liberated.

20, SOLOMON PENDLETON, belonging to the State of New York with a pass from Justice Van Tassel of Winchester, York State.

March 3, MAGNUS MILLER, } just arrived in this City after
WILLIAM MILLER, } absence of near eight years.

8, MARTIN HENRY SHOLTZ, a Prussian, deserted the Brittish Army about 4 years. Breeches Maker.

14, ANDREW ALBERS (his mark), of the Regt. of Reidezel, a Prussian, late prisoner of war liberated.

15, JOHN PIGISSON, seaman, made his escape from the Midstone Frigate at N. York.

April 1, JONATHAN DAVIS, of the County Cumberland, State of N. Jersey. Turner.

DANIEL SMITH, of said County & State. Carpenter.

3, ALEXANDER SHLOTMAN, a Hessian deserted from the Enemy at Rhode Island in 1779.

May 12, MARTIN SHETLER } Germans born, deserted the
(his mark), } Brittish Army at Long Island
MARTIN HAGER, } the 25th of April last.

16, JOHN CLAUDE LAODIE, deserted the Hessian Army, served with the French General & discharged.

1783.

May 28, JOHANNES STAIN BAUGH, ⎫ lately deserted the ene-
JUSTICE FLOAK, ⎬ my & Hessian Line
WILHELM RUDOLPH, ⎭ from New York.

June 5, JOHN KEYS, being taken prisoner & forced into the Brittish Service in 1782, deserted the Man of War last week.

JAMES NEVIL (his mark), formerly of Maryland, taken prisoner by the Brittish at sea, was forced into the Brittish Service & deserted the man of war last week.

9, JOHANNES SHUGHART, ⎫ deserted the Brittish Army
JACOB BAUMGART, ⎬ & Hessian Line at New York.

12, JAMES DELANY, lately from Ireland.

17, A. J. DALLAS, from the Island of Jamaica.
JOHN BENTLEY, Idem.

19, JOHN NASSAU, a native of Philada., but pressed into the Brittish Sea Service.

(THOMAS BELL, late apprentice), see Oath of 1778.

20, PARRY HALL, Printer.

21, BOGEN, DOCTR. ⎫ Late of the Hessian Line & lately
GROSSE, DOCTR. ⎬ from New York, being discharged.

24, CHARLES CRAWFORD, Barrister at Law, lately arrived in this City, from Antigua via New York.

25, JOHAN MARTIN HENDERICH, of the Hessian Line, lately from New York. Joyner.

July 11, JAMES MACOMBE, Mercht., late of London last from New York.

Aug. 18, STEWART GEORGE DALLAS, lately arrived from Jamaica. Attorney at Law.

1783.
Aug. 19, JAMES CARROLL (his mark), Seaman for some years.
 21, JOHN QUINLEN, formerly in the Sea Service, late Captain of the Privateer Brigg Halker.
 MARTIN MAHER, lately arrived in this City from Martinique via Boston.
 27, JOHANN GROBEY, of Anspach, lately deserted the Brittish at New York.
Sept. 10, HENRY CARLISLE, lately from Ireland, a house Carpenter well recommended.
 11, JOHANNES EBERT, deserted from the Hessian Army & resident in this state three years.
 18, ALEXANDER STEWART, lately deserted the Brittish Army at New York.
 24, HENRY WEEKES, formerly in the Brittish Service.
Oct. 9, JOHN MARSAN, a native of France. Mercht.
 14, JAMES JOHNSTON, a soldier discharged, made proof that he took the Oath of Allegiance in 1777.
 GEORGE MEADE, took the Oath in 1777 as by testimony appears.
 ZACHARIAH LESH, proves that he took the test before me in 1777.
 ROBERT MORRELL, an artificer in the American Service, discharged.
 EDWARD WHELAN, a soldier in Pennsylvania Line, discharged.
 ROBERT TAYLOR, of Philada. made proof that he took the test in 1777 before me.
 ROBERT SMITH, of Philada. took the test June 27 1777 before me.

1783.

Oct. 14, JAMES AMES, of Philada. Blacksmith, proves that on the 31st July 1777 he took the Oath of Allegiance before me.

Nov. 3, CHARLES HUNTER, lately arrived in this City from Hampshire in Britain. Bricklayer.

21, JOHN VEDER, lately arrived in this City, a Native of Rotterdam. Mariner.

28, JOHANNES CRESS, lately arrived here from Amsterdam, a Baker by trade.

Dec. 1, JOHN ADAM SEITZ, lately from Germany, by trade a Miller.

5, ALBERT WARNICK, deserted the Brittish Army at New York. Sadler.

DAVID TURNER, late a prisoner of the Brittish Army in this City, discharged.

8, ZEMAN THOMAS REDE, Barrister at Law, lately arrived in this City from London.

JOHN DAVAN, Merchant, arrived in this City with his family about 4 weeks from Dublin.

15, JACOB LAHN, lately at Baltimore from Amsterdam. Linguister.

GEORGE BENDER, a Hessian lately deserted from New York. Taylor.

FREDERICK MOLINEUX, of Philada. Mercht., took the Oath of Allegiance 31st Augt. 1777.

1784.

Jan. 23, LEWIS HALLAM, lately arrived from Jamaica.

31, WILLIAM THOMPSON, lately from Ireland. Mercht.

Feb. 10, ISRAEL GOETTE, } Hessians lately
LOEDWICK HUVORT (his mark), } from New York.

1784,

March 1, PETER BARRIERE, a native of France. Mercht.

 5, JOHN HAMILTON, of Pennsylva., lately from London. Attorney at Law.

 22, PETER MARKOE, Gentleman, lately arrived in this City from the Island Santa Cruz.

April 8, FELIX BRUNOT, native of France & a resident in this City three years. Hair Dresser.

 12, JOHANNES FISHER, a Hessian formerly in the Brittish Service.

 THOMAS WHITE, formerly of the Brittish Army, now resident in this City. Shoemaker.

 RICHARD HOWELL, Attorney at Law, a resident of the Jersey State.

 14, THOMAS CARSTAIRS, lately from London. House Carpenter.

 15, JOSEPH ALLENSPACHERN, lately from Germany. Clockmaker.

 21, JOHN MCINTOSH, lately arrived from Scotland.

 JAMES WILLIAMSON,   same.

May 28, JOHN D. HAUSSMAN, a Dantzicker, lately from London. Mercht.

June 14, ARCHIBALD BLEAKLY, lately arrived from Ireland, says about 15 months. Mercht.

 17, JOHN ROOF, late of the County of Bucks. Blacksmith.

 ISAAC FRANK.

 HENRY GREER, late Lieut. of the 4th Pennsa. Regt.

 DAVID RITTENHOUSE, affirmed that in 1777, he took & subscribed as by law required.

 29, JOSEPH DE LA CROIX, a native of France, arrived here in January last.

1784.

June 30, CHARLES VAN ECKHENT, a Hollander by birth, bred in France & resident in America 4 years.

(REV.) JOHN CAMPBELL, of the Episcopal Church, lately arrived in this City from London.

July 5, STEPHEN SICARD, a native of France & a resident in this State 18 months.

JAN CHRISTIAN BRUYN, Cook, of Saxe Gothia resident here one year.

FREDERICK WILLIAM WINCKLER, Farmer, late of Germany & resident here six months.

8, GOTTLIEB KINDER, a German in the Brittish Service, deserted from Long Island.

14, JOSEPH HARRISON, formerly a subject of Britain lately from Charlestown. Mercht.

THOMAS VICKERS, formerly in the Brittish Service, lately arrived in Philada. Taylor.

19, JEAN KROP, a German discharged from the French Army, by trade a Joyner.

Aug. 6, CHRISTIAN GOTTLIEB BEMÉ, a Saxon, a resident 3 years in America.

18, MAXIMILIAN LOUIS ALEXANDRE DE CRESSY, a native of France & resident in Philada. one year. Mercht.

24, JOSEPH HONAKER, of Moyamensing, & a Native of this State. Lately come to the age of 21 years.

Sept. 28, VINCENZO MARIA PELOSI, arrived in this City about a year past. Mercht.

Oct. 1, EDWARD ALLEN, Mercht., arrived about five months from Jamaica.

JOHN PHILLIPS, hairdresser, left Philada. in 1776 & returned in 1783.

1784.

Oct. 1, GUY BRYAN, arrived in this City from England in Septr. 1783. Mercht.

WILLIAM FALKENER, Mercht., arrived in Philada. in March last from England.

5, WILLIAM STILES, arrived in this City from London above one year.

7, ROGER PRESCOTT, Mercht., arrived in this City from London in Febry. 1784.

8, WILLIAM CAVENOUGH, Conveyancer, took the Oath in Virginia in 1778.

9, JOHN LENTZ (his mark), son of Henry Lentz of Moyamensing, lately arrived to age.

JONATHAN WORRELL, Cabinet Maker, took the Oath in 1777 as appears by Certificate worn out.

CALEB EVANS, son of David Evans of this City, lately arrived to Age.

JAMES HALL, a native of Moreland lately arrived to full age.

DANIEL BOINOD, a foreigner resident of this City a full year.

ALEXANDER GAILLARD, resident as above.

DAVID EVERHARD, Butcher, made Oath that he took the Oath of Allegiance in 1777.

11, JOHN GUIER, son of Adam Guier of Kingsessing, lately come of age.

ROBT. SMITH JUNR., son of Robt. Smith, lately come to age.

BENJAMIN ROGERS, a Native lately arrived to the age of 21 years. Shoemaker.

12, PETER REINHARD, Son of Martin Reinhard of

1784.

Passiunk, lately come to age of 21 years. Wheelwright.

Oct. 12, PETER STANLEY, son of the late Vale. Stanley of Philada., a freeholder.

BARTHOLOMEW SIMS, a native of Chester County, served Apprenticeship in this City, now 21 years of Age.

PETER FIELD, makes Oath that he took the Oath agreeable to Law in 1777.

JACOB GARAND, of Philada. Taylor.

JOHN SADLER, a native of Philada. lately come to age of twenty one years.

ANDREW SPENCE, Dentist, arrived in this City from London in July last.

JAMES HOGGEN, late of the State of New York, a resident in this City above three years.

ROBERT WATTS, of Philada. Cooper, made Oath that in 1777 in Bucks County he gave the test of Allegiance.

FREDERICK ESLING, son of Paul Esling of Philada., a native come to age of 21 years.

WILLIAM LEVERING, son of William of Roxbury, lately come to the age of 21.

JACOB MILLER, lately arrived to full age. A native of Germantown.

FREDERICK DOVER, a native of Philada. lately come to the age of 21.

JAMES TOD, arrived in this City from Edinburgh in Septr. 1783. Teacher of Languages.

THOMAS CRAIG, took the Oath in 1777 & had a Certificate which is lost.

1784.

Oct. 12, BENJAMIN ENGLE, a native of Germantown near 21 years of age.

PHILIP PELTZ, a native of Passiunk, now 21 years of age.

WILLIAM LOCKHART, arrived from Ireland, resident in this City above one year.

JACOB CUBLER (his mark), } natives of Passiunk & lately of the age of 21 years.
PHILIP YOUNG (his mark),

JOSHUA VANDEGRIFT, a native of Bucks County, lately come to the age of 21.

JOSEPH KEEN, a native of Philadelphia lately come to age.

CHARLES TODD, took the Oath in Maryland in 1777, resident 3 years in this City.

WILLIAM BROWN, arrived in this City from England near two years past.

NICHOLAUS DILL, formerly a Soldier in the Contl. Army & State of New York, a native of this City.

GEORGE DEAMAND, of Philada., Taylor, makes Oath that he took the Oath in 1777.

FRANCIS CUMFORT (his mark), a Seaman, has resided here two years.

THOMAS CLARK, resident in this city 4 years & lately come to full age.

WILLIAM MILLER, a native of Maryland & resident here above two years.

JAMES WILLIAMS, a native of Philada., took the Oath of Allegiance in Charlestown in 1778.

1784.

Oct. 12, FREDERICK JUDE, a residenter in Philada. from a Child, lately come to the age of 21 years.

ALEXANDER NIMMO, resident a full year. Shoemaker from Scotland.

THOMAS MCCULLEY, makes oath that he took the test of N. Jersey in 1778.

CORNELIUS BRADLEY (his mark), in servitude in 1778, lately arrived to the age of 25 years.

DONALD MCDONALD, a resident of Philada. who neglected to take the test in due time.

PETER VICTOR DOREY, a native of France, resident here above one year.

HENRY DETTERLINE, a native of Bucks County lately come to the age of 21 years.

ISAAC COATS, a native of the Northern Liberties, now 23 years of age.

JOHN LETCHWORTH, from England, resident here 15 years, lately come to full age.

WILLIAM YOUNG, son of a Freeholder of this City, late come to 21 years of age.

THOMAS A. MORRIS, from Ireland, resident above one year.

MATTHEW BROOKE, native of Philada. County, resident in this City lately. Affirmed.

JOSEPH MERCIER, a Foreigner, resident in this City three years. Mercht.

Nov. 22, JOHN CONRAD MITS, Wine Mercht. arrived in this City about 2 years past from Lubeck.

Dec. 9, JOHN CHILD, house Carpenter arrived in this City near two years past from England.

1784.
Dec. 13, JAMES BERWICK, late Lieut. in the Army of the United States, made Oath that in the year 1778 before Justice Hubley of Lancr., he did take & subscribe allegiance as by Law directed.
    17, (CAPT.) WILLIAM PINKERTON, of the Ship William & George.
    27, CHARLES PALESKE, lately arrived here from Dantzig. Mercht.

1785.
April 30, WILLIAM HEALY, Silver Plater, arrived from Dublin in November last.
May 9, WILLIAM NATHANIEL SWAIN, lately arrived in this City from Ireland.
    18, CARL DE DEKE, lately arrived from Germany, penmaker.
June 17, HENRY KESLER (his mark), a German, a resident of this state about six years.
    25, RICHARD LAKE, doctor of Law, lately arrived in this City from the kingdom of Scotland.
    JAMES STEVENS, arrived in this City about ten months from England. Mercht.
July 20, JAMES PRIDE, arrived here from Scotland in August last. Chandler.
    25, ZACHARIAH LOURIETTE, Mercht., from France, having resided here above eighteen months.
Aug. 9, JOSEPH ASHWORTH a native of Virginia. Farmer.
    17, CAPT. LEWIS GARANGER, a native of France, resident here & in the service of the States nine years.
    23, JOSHUA BYRON, from England, Mercht., says he has resided here above two years.

1785.

Aug. 23, THOMAS SEDDON, from England, Mercht., says he has resided here above two years.

25, HANDY PEMBERTON, (affirmed,) Barrister at Law, Lately arrived from Dublin.

Sept. WILLIAM JACKSON MCKENZIE, lately from Ireland. Mercht.

THOMAS O'NEILL, lately from Ireland. Mercht.

15, WILLIAM HUGH, Breeches maker, from Scotland, says above one year past.

26, JOHN DAVIS, Upholsterer.

JAMES KING, from Virginia, late of New York. Mercht.

29, LLOYD WHARTON, a native of this City lately come to the age of 21 years.

Oct. 8, PATRICK CONNELLY, says he was a Sergeant in the Maryland Line, was taken prisoner & inlisted in the Brittish Service & deserted from them in the year 1781.

WILLIAM YOUNG, Stationer, arrived in this City from Scotland in June 1784.

(ANNANIAS COOPER), swore allegiance 30th June 1777 as appears by a broken certificate.

GEORG KOOPER, proves that he took the test in 1777 & hath lost his certificate.

EDWARD MOYSTON, a foreigner, resident in this City above five years.

GEORGE MOORE, from Ireland, resident in this City near two years.

RICHARD PARKER, a native of this City lately come to full age.

1785.

Oct. 8, JOHN SELLERS JUNR., lately arrived to the age of 21 years.

THOMAS STEEL, son of David Steel, lately arrived to the age of 21 years.

THOMAS HOOD.

JAMES RONEY, from Ireland, arrived here about 18 months.

10, ABRAHAM KINTZING JUNR., a native of Philada. lately come to age.

EPHRAIM FERGUSON, from Ireland, resident in this City above one year.

ABSALOM THOMAS, a native of Bucks County, lately arrived in to full age.

JOHN CARRIN, maketh oath that he took the Oath in Cumberland Co. before Squire Loughlin in the year 1777.

JOSIAH W. GIBBS, came from Boston in the year 1779.

PETER BAYNTON, made Oath that he took Oath before me in 1777.

MATTHEW GRAHAM, made Oath that he took the Oath before me in 1777.

JOSEPH THOMAS, of Lower Dublin, lately come to full age. Affirmed.

WM. DONOVAN, from Ireland, resident of this City about two years.

PETER SCRAVENDYKE, Tallow Chandler, from Ireland, resident of this City two years.

WILLIAM COLLINS, Carpenter, from Ireland, resident here near two years.

1785.

Oct. 10, PETER WHITE, a native of this City, tinman, lately come to full age.

JOHN BRUNSTRONG from Sweden, resident here about 4 years.

11, JOSEPH MAFFETT (his mark), served apprentice in this City, lately of full age.

CHRISTOPHER SPITTER, a German, resident here near two years.

JOHN LACKRUM, makes Oath that he took the test in 1777.

JAMES RYAN, from Ireland, resident in this city above one year.

ALEXANDER MCDONALD, from Scotland, resident above one year.

SAMUEL SIMES, from London, resident above one year.

MARTIN KUBLER, lately come of age.

ECCLES BUCHANAN, from Ireland, resident here near two years.

SAMUEL LOWREY, of the Jersey State, lately arrived to full age.

JAMES WADE, native of Philada., lately come to full age.

THOMAS RANDALL, from London, resident here two years.

HENRY TOWN, a native of Philada., lately come to full age.

JOHN JOHNSON, from Ireland, resident here near two years.

GEORGE WHITE, from England, resident here near two years.

1785.

Oct. 11, JACOB ECKSTEIN, served apprenticeship here & lately come of full age.

JOSEPH LAMBETH, from England, resident here near two years.

ROBERT BREARLY, from England, resident here four years.

WILLIAM MCDERMOTT, from the Jersey State, where he took the Oath of Allegiance in 1777.

JOHN WILLSON (his mark), from Ireland, served apprentice in Chester Co. lately come to full age.

FREDERICK BURKHARD (his mark), a native, served apprentice in Philada., of age near 4 years.

JOHN WALRAVIN, a native of the Delaware State.

JACOB TAYLOR (his mark), a native of Philada., lately come to full age.

E. DOUGLASS, of Philada., Mercht., native of Penna., resident here 4 years & lately come to full age.

JOHN GODSHALL, of Philada., now 25 years of age.

SAMUEL HARKNESS, from Ireland, resident here above one year.

ALEXANDER SYMINGTON, from Scotland, resident above two years.

WILLIAM RICHARDSON, from Ireland, resident here above one year.

RICHARD DENNY, a native of Philada., now 22 years of age.

TIMOTHY RYAN, from Ireland, resident here near 27 years.

CHURCH CLINTON, from Ireland, resident above one year.

1785.

Oct. 11, GILBERT GAA, a native, resident in Philada. where he served apprentice, lately of full age.

THOMAS MAYSEY, took the test in Jersey in 1777 & now before me.

BENJAMIN MCELROY, served apprentice in this City, late come to full age.

CHRISTIAN TULLON (his mark), from Germany when young, since resident of this State & lately come to age.

GODFREY TULLON (his mark), same.

CONRAD ROUN, took the test in New York in 1777 & now before me.

DANIEL PENINGTON, proves that he took the Oath before Justice Denci of Bucks Co. in the beginning of 1778.

EPHRAIM BROWN, makes Oath that he took the test in Rhode Island & now before me.

MAURICE DICKINSON.

DUNCAN MONTGOMERY, from Scotland, resident here above one year.

JOHN HUDSON, from the State of Virginia, resident in this City about 1 year.

WILLIAM SMITH, a native of Philada., lately come to full age.

JOHN GALVAN.

JAMES GARDETTE, from France, a resident in this City above one year.

ISRAEL ISRAEL, with Certificate from the Delaware State.

JAMES ROBERTS, took the test in Maryland in 1780 & now before me.

1785.

Oct. 11, THOMAS BREHNERT (his mark), from England near 2 years.

JOHN BAES, a foreigner, resident in this City near two years.

GEORGE HARMAN, a native of Philada., lately come to full age.

CONRAD GARRETT (his mark), a soldier in the Penna. Line discharged on the peace.

GEORGE HARMAN, a native of this City, now of full age.

WILLIAM M. BIDDLE, a native of Philada., lately of full age.

JOHN LYNCH, a native of Virginia, resident in this City 2 years.

MARKS JOHN BIDDLE, a native of Philada., lately come to full age.

JOHN GOODMAN, a Native of Philada. Co., resident of Philada., lately come to full age. Affirmed.

JOHN MCKINSEY, from Scotland, resident here one year.

JACOB LOWDEN, a native of this City, lately of full age.

PHILIP DEFRANCQUEN, from France, resident in this City above one year.

ABRAHAM BOYER, a native of Philada. County, resident of this City & lately of full age.

JOSEPH DAVIS, a native of Philada., son of a freeholder & of full age.

JAMES MACKAY (his mark), a native of Philada., lately come to full age.

1785.

Dec. 8, JOHN RICHARDS JUNR., Mercht., last from France, resident in this City above three years.

27, WILLIAM P. HARRISON, arrived in this City October 1784. Printer.

CARSTEN WINCKEL, lately arrived in this City from Amsterdam. Ship Carpenter.

1786.

Jan. 7, PETER LIGAUX, a native of France, lately from the West Indies.

Feb. 3, JOHN SAINTON, arrived in this City from Corsica about three years past.

FRANÇOIS SERRE, arrived in this City from France above two years.

VINCENT DUCOMB, arrived in this City from France above two years past.

HENRY STERNBAK, a German, arrived in this City near two years past.

March 17, ROBERT BUNTIN, a native of Ireland, resident in this City about 8 years.

April 3, JACQUE SALLIER, from France, resident here above two years. Taylor.

12, JOHN CRAWFORD, from Ireland, resident here above three years.

May 8, DAVID CLARK, from Scotland, resident near one year. Coachmaker.

ROBERT NICOL, from Scotland, Coach Maker, resident here near two years.

THOMAS LANG, from Scotland, resident here near two years.

JOHN FINETON, from Scotland, Carpenter, resident here above one year.

1786.

May 8, JOHN DUN, from Scotland, Carpenter, resident here near one year.

JOHN ANDERSON, from Scotland, resident in this State one year.

JOHN NICOLSON, from Scotland, storekeeper, resident in this City near two years.

ROBERT JOHNSTON, from Scotland, Baker, resident of this State near two years.

ROBERT OSWALD, from Scotland, House Carpenter, resident here above one year.

JAMES COWAN, from Scotland, blacksmith, resident here above six months.

ANDREW DUFFUS, from Scotland, Shoemaker, resident in this City Eighteen months.

BENJAMIN JAMES, late of London, Mercht., resident in this City above two years.

June 6, ANDREW WERREBROUEK, late of Flanders, Mercht., resident here near one year.

7, PETER L. CAILLEAU, late of Flanders, Mercht., lately arrived in this City.

July 11, ROBERT E. PINE, late of London, Painter, resident here about 2 years.

12, JEAN BAPTISTE LEMAIRE, Mercht., from French Flanders, resident here above one year.

ADRIEN JOSEPH LUBRER, from French Flanders, Mercht., lately arrived in this City.

Aug. 29, NICOLA MANSAI, hatmaker, arrived here from France one year past.

Sept. 2, THOMAS RYAN, breeches maker, from Ireland, arrived in this City about two years.

1786.

Sept. 23, JAMES REES, of Philada., lately arrived to full age.

26, BENJAMIN H. SMITH, of the Township of Blockley, lately arrived to full age. Affirmed.

30, THOMAS HURLEY, arrived in this City from Ireland above two years past.

Oct. 3, GEORGE RUDOLPH, of Philada., Rope Maker, lately arrived to full age.

JOSEPH HODGSON, a native of the Delaware State, hatter, now near 20 years of age.

JOSEPH KRESSON, of this City, Rope Maker, a freeholder, lately come to age.

JAMES STEWART, arrived in this City from Ireland about two years, by trade a blacksmith.

JOHN SNYDER, maketh Oath that in the year 1777 he took the Oath as by law directed before me.

CHRISTOPHER FORD, Wheelwright, a Native of the City, lately come to Age.

ROBERT PAISLEY, swears that at Bristol in Bucks County, he gave test of his allegiance in 1777.

DAVID MCCALL (his mark), blacksmith, arrived in this City from Ireland about two years.

9, LEONARD ALTEMUS, Taylor, a native of Philada., lately come to full age.

JAMES ANDERSON, of Philada. Mariner, proves that he took the Oath in 1777 & had a certificate.

JOSEPH MUSSI, from Italy, arrived in this City two years past.

JOHN SUMMERS, Shoemaker, arrived in this City from Scotland two years past.

1786.

Oct. 10, BENJAMIN HARBESON JUNR., Mercht., lately come to age.

PETER THOMAS, Trader, arrived in this City from France above one year past.

FREDERICK HYNEMAN, by his Certificate shows that he took the test 30 June 1777.

ROBERT K. MOORE, of Philada., Mercht., lately arrived to full age.

WILLIAM FORGEY, Taylor, arrived in this City from Ireland three years past.

THOMAS ALBERTSON, of Philada., Skindresser, lately come to full age.

THOMAS SISSON, Conveyancer, arrived in this City from England above two years.

LEWIS EVANS of this City, silversmith, lately of full age.

CHRISTOPHER SMITH, proves he took the test in 1777.

JONATHAN SMITH JUNR., of Philada., Gent., lately arrived to full age.

GEORGE SMITH, Currier, arrived in America from Scotland above one year.

PHILIP DUNN, native of Philada., lately come to full age.

JACOB WONDERLY, of Philada., Butcher, lately come to full age.

WILLIAM OWENS, house carpenter, arrived in this City from Ireland above two years.

JABEZ EMORY, came to this City from Maryland when he took the test, resident here above 2 years.

1786.
Oct. 10, ALEXANDER GRANT, House Carpenter, arrived here from Scotland above two years.

ROBERT BLACKIE, blacksmith, come to this City above two years past.

WILLIAM SOTHERN, of this City, Mariner, resident here above one year.

ROBERT LUMSDEN, of Philada., Taverner, proves that he took the test in 1777.

ELIAS BOYS JUNR., of Southwark, a native lately of full age.

MANUEL ANTONY, native of Spain, Mariner, resident here five years.

THOMAS WYNN, of the Township of Blockley, lately come to Age.

JOHN CAROTHERS, taylor, arrived in this City about three years past.

CHAS. McKIERNAN, Mercht., arrived in this City from Ireland full twelve months.

PATRICK GLYN, Taylor, arrived in this City above two years past.

OLIVER POLLOCK, of this City, Gent., arrived here from Havana near 2 years.

DAVID NEWEL (his mark), of Northern Liberties, lately come to full age.

JOSEPH JORDON, of the Northern Liberties, Plasterer, a Native lately come to full age.

JAMES HOOFMAN (his mark), of the Northern Liberties, Turner, lately come to full age.

MICHAEL HAINES, of the Northern Liberties, lately come to full age.

1786.
Oct. 10, JOHN MINGLE, of the Northern Liberties, Blacksmith, lately come to full age.

JOHN KINSEL, of the Northern Liberties, Blacksmith, native, lately of full age.

CADWALADER GRIFFITH, Shoemaker, lately come to full age.

LAURENCE LOTIE, barber, arrived in this City from France about 5 years past.

CHARLES DE GROFEY, Mercht., arrived here from France above three years past.

PETER ANDREWS, Cordwainer, a native of this City, lately come to full age.

WILLIAM BANDONINE, a native of New York, resident of this City two years, lately of full age.

JOHN FITZSIMONS, came to this City from Ireland about two years past.

WILLIAM FERGUSON, arrived here where he has resided near three years.

NICHOLAS HESS, Blacksmith, a Native of this State, lately of full age.

JOHN HESS, Blacksmith, a native of this State, lately of full age.

ELSHA HAGUE, a Native of Philada., lately come to full age.

12, JULIUS MANER, late a Hessian Soldier who hath served three years in the Army.

1787.
Jan. 31, JAMES YARD, a Native of this State, lately of full age.

1787.

March 3, THOMAS CRAIG, arrived in this City from Ireland in the year 1783, by trade a House Carpenter.

May 7, WILLIAM CUNNINGHAM, Stone Cutter, came to the City from London in the year 1783.

Sept. 6, ANGUS TAYLOR, Shoemaker, arrived in this City from Scotland above two years.

1788.

Sept. 19, GEORGE GREER, arrived in this City from Ireland in the year 1784.

23, JOHN BRIGGS, Glover, lately from London.

27, THOMAS COATS, Clock & Watch Maker, arrived in this City from Scotland in 1788.

Oct. 11, WILLIAM ANDERSON, of this City, hair dresser, who took the Oath of Allegiance in 1777.

13, FREDERICK CONYNGHAM, arrived in this City in Septr. 1787. Mercht.

14, JOHN SIMTER, formerly a Dragoon in the Service of the United States.

JOHN EBALT, late a Soldier in the American Army.

INDEX TO HISTORY.

	PAGE
Adams, John, his resolution in favor of creating independent State Governments	xiii
Afflick, Thomas, arrested	xxi
Allegiance—Oaths and declarations of—For the support of British Government denounced by Congress—Grand Jurors' oath incompatible with opposition to the King	xiii
Religious test adopted	xiv
Justices of Peace oaths of renunciation and allegiance—Religious test for members of the State Assembly—Objections to it	xv
Testimony of Quakers against the test, December, 1776	xvi
State Navy Board refuses to take oath of allegiance to State—Offer to take oath in favor of United States	xvi
Test and oath of allegiance of 1777	xvii
Preamble to the act—Form of the oath	xviii
Penalties against persons who will not take the oath	xix
Whigs flock in to take the oath	xx
Time for taking oath extended	xxiii
Persons in certain professions prohibited from following them without taking the oath—Penalty for not taking the oath	xxiv
Protests of Quakers against the oath	xxv
Further extension of time to take the oath—Pardon of persons pertinaciously refusing to take the oath, 1778	xxvi
Opposition of Quakers to the test, 1779	xxvii
Proposition to abolish test laws, 1784, lost—Resolution to allow young men who arrived at 18 years since the passage of the law to take the oath—Referred to a committee	xxxiii
Non-jurors petition for rights of citizenship, referred—Proposition to exclude from citizenship all who aided the King of Great Britain in the late war, carried—Proposition to bring in a bill to entitle any one to take the oath of allegiance, carried—attempt to pass the bill—breaking up of the Assembly—nineteen members secede	xxxiv
Protest of the seceders—George Gray's (Speaker) address against seceders—reasons why test laws should be repealed	xxxv
Petitions by Non-jurors, 1785—General Anthony Wayne favors them,	xxxvi
Committee appointed—Bitter report against the Non-jurors	xxxvii
Arguments in favor of the oath—The report adopted—New petition of Non-jurors, 1785	xxxviii
Executive Council recommends abolition of the test laws—passage of Act of 1786 limited in terms	xxxix
Dissatisfaction of the Non-jurors—Remonstrances in 1787—Report of committee in favor of unconditional repeal—passage of an amended act—Quakers dissatisfied with it—Proceedings against two Grand Jurors	xl

Q

	PAGE
Allegiance—Report in favor of repeal, 1788	xli
Final repeal of the test laws—Religious test in Constitution of 1776 repealed by Constitution of 1790	xlii
See also "Quakers," "Tories," "Associators."	
Allen, Andrew, attainted	xxiii
Allen, Jno., attainted	xxiii
Asheton, Thos., arrested	xxi
Ashmead, Samuel, candidate for Assembly, favorable to Non-jurors, 1784, defeated	xxxvi
Assembly of Pennsylvania under the crown—Distrusted at the commencement of the Revolution—Authorizes raising troops	vii
Measures taken to supersede it	xiii
Its dying protest	xiv, xv
Assembly of the State under the new Constitution	xv
Meets at Lancaster	xxii
Interrogatories to a committee of Quakers	xxiv
Queries to Quakers petitioning against test laws in 1779	xxvii
Unsatisfactory reply	xxviii
Broken up in 1784 upon attempt to pass laws for relief of Non-jurors	xxxiv
See "Allegiance," "Quakers."	
Associators—Volunteer militia	viii, ix
Dissatisfied with Assembly in 1776—Protest against allowing Assembly to choose their Generals—Circulars issued calling Convention at Lancaster	xii
Brigadier-Generals elected	xiii
In favor of suppressing old Provincial Assembly—Conference at Carpenter's Hall—Provincial Convention to form Constitution recommended—Religious test adopted	xiv
Not reliable troops—Desertions when at Amboy—City Troop at Princeton, N. J.—Superseded by militia under a general law	xvii
Attainder Act of 1778	xxii
Bergum, John, his recantation	viii
Biddle, John, attainted	xxiii
Bond, Phineas, arrested	xxi
Brown, Elijah, arrested	xxi
Byberry—Scarcity of persons who had taken the oath, 1785	xxxviii
Coats, William, elected to Assembly on anti-Non-juror ticket, 1784	xxxvi
College and Academy at Philadelphia—Charter taken away	xxii
Committees—City and County—Manage local affairs at beginning of Revolution	vii, viii
Committee of Inspection, Philadelphia, attack the authority of the King's Judges	xiii
Coombe, Rev. Thomas, arrested	xxi
Permitted to go to St. Eustatia	xxii
Confiscation of traitors' estates authorized	xxiii
Congress recommends formation of State Governments	xiii
Convention to frame Constitution—Proceedings of, 1776	xiv
Council of Safety appointed	xiv
Crathorne, Joseph, a Tory, ordered to leave Pennsylvania	xxxii
Drinker, Henry, arrested	xxi
Duché, Rev Jacob Jr, attainted	xxiii

INDEX TO HISTORY. 123

	PAGE
Eddy, Charles, arrested	xxi
Emlen, Caleb, arrested—Took the oath	xxi
Emlen, Samuel, Jr., arrested	xxi
Ewing, James, elected Brigadier-General	xiii
Faro, Lancelot, a Tory, ordered to leave Pennsylvania	xxxii
Faro, Thomas, a Tory, ordered to leave Pennsylvania	xxxii
Fenner, Lawrence, a Tory, ordered to leave Pennsylvania	xxxii
Fisher, Jabez Maud, compelled to state who wrote a certain letter	viii
Fisher, Joshua, arrested	xxi
Fisher, Miers, arrested	xxi
Fisher, Thomas, arrested	xxi
Fitzsimons, Thomas, candidate for Assembly, favorable to Non-jurors 1784, defeated	xxxvi
Fouts, Christian, attainted	xxiii
Fox, Joseph, arrested	xxi
Francis, Tench, attorney for the Penn family, applies for restoration of their rights	xxxv
Franklin, Benjamin, President Convention to form State Constitution	xiv
President Supreme Executive Council—Recommended abolition of the test laws, 1785	xxxix
Fleeson, Plunket, Commissioner to receive oaths of allegiance	xxvi
Friends, see "Quakers."	
Galloway, Joseph, attainted	xxiii
Garrigues, Jacob, Assistant Secretary Convention to form State Constitution	xiv
Gibbons, Abraham, one of a Committee of Quakers	xxiv
Gilpin, Thomas, arrested	xxi
Dies in exile in Virginia	xxvi
Gratz, Bernard, of Jewish Congregation, protests against religious test	xxxii
Gray, George, Speaker of the Assembly, 1784—Censures the seceders	xxxv
Halliday, Robert, of Duck Creek, writes an obnoxious letter	viii
Hart, Joseph, Vice President State Conference	xiv
Hicks, Gilbert, attainted	xxiii
Howell, Isaac, Commissioner to receive oaths of allegiance	xxvi
Hunt, John, arrested	xxi
Dies in exile in Virginia	xxvi
Husband, Joseph, one of a Committee of Quakers	xxiv
Imlay, William, arrested	xxi
Released on parole	xxii
Jackson, James, one of a Committee of Quakers	xxiv
Jackson, Samuel, ordered to be arrested—Not found	xxi
Jackson, William Jr., one of a Committee of Quakers	xxiv
James, Abel, arrested	xxi
James, John, ordered to be arrested—Not found	xxi
Jervis, Charles, arrested	xxi
Jews—Protest against religious test in acknowledging the New Testament, 1783	xxxii
Jones, Norris, Quaker Grand Juryman, fined	xli
Jones, Owen, Jr., arrested	xxi

	PAGE
Juncken, Herr, his recantation	ix
Justices of Peace appointed	xv
Keen, Reynold, attainted	xxiii
Knox, David, Commissioner to receive oaths of allegiance	xxvi
Kuhn, Dr. Adam, arrested—Produced proof that he had taken the oath—discharged	xxi
Lennot, William, arrested	xxi
Lennox, David, arrested	xxi
Levy, Mordecai, his recantation	viii
Lindley, Jacob, one of a Committee of Quakers	xxiv
Loosely, Thomas, is "exalted"	viii
McKean, Thomas, President State Conference	xiv
Chief Justice, fines two Quakers who had not taken the affirmation of allegiance	xl, xli
Marshall, Christopher, extract from his diary	viii
Matlack, Timothy, Secretary of Committee of Inspection	ix
Mifflin, Warner, one of a Committee of Quakers	xxiv
Miles, Col. Samuel, Chairman of a meeting against Tories, 1783	xxx
Militia law of 1777	xvii
Mitchell, James, a Tory, ordered to leave Pennsylvania	xxxii
Moderates agree with the views of the Tories	xiii
Moor, John, Commissioner to receive oaths of allegiance	xxvi
Morris, John, Secretary Convention to form State Constitution	xiv
Morris, Robert, his amendment to Act modifying test laws in 1786	xxxix
Morris, Samuel Cadwalader, Secretary State Conference	xiv
Murdock, Samuel, arrested	xxi
Myers, Asher, of Jewish Congregation, protests against religious test	xxxii
Nathan, Simon, President Jewish Synagogue, protests against religious test	xxxii
Oath—See "Allegiance."	
Ord, George, Commissioner to receive oaths of allegiance	xxvi
Ozeas, Peter, begs pardon for increasing price of coffee	ix
Pemberton, Israel, arrested	xxi
Pemberton, James, arrested	xxi
Pemberton, John, arrested	xxi
Penn, John, Senr., applies for restoration of his rights	xxxv
Penn, John, Jr., applies for restoration of his rights	xxxv
Penn, Richard, applies for restoration of his rights	xxxv
Pennington, Edward, arrested	xxi
Pettit, Charles, elected to Assembly on anti-Non-juror ticket, 1781	xxxvi
Pike, Thomas, arrested	xxi
Pleasants, Samuel, arrested	xxi
Potter, John, attainted	xxiii
Putnam, Gen. Israel, his testimony as to inefficiency of Associators	xvii
Quakers, opposed to war and favor the Royal cause	v
Lose their power in Pennsylvania	vi

	PAGE
Quakers—Testimony in favor of the King's Government, 1776—Satire upon American liberty in 1776	x
Testimony against tests and in favor of the King's Government, December, 1776	xvi
Complaints of seizures of their goods for military purposes—Their windows broken because they will not recognize public fast days—Abused because they would not illuminate their houses on the 4th of July—Quakers and Tories arrested by order of Congress	xx
Sent to Winchester, Va.	xxi
A committee ask leave to lay their sufferings before Assembly	xxiv
Queries as to their loyalty—Evasive reply—Protest by, against oath of allegiance	xxv
Petition for return of exiles in Virginia	xxv
Release and return of the persons who were banished	xxvi
Testimony of 1779 against the test laws—Memorial to the Assembly—Queries put by Assembly to the Quakers regarding their loyalty	xxvii
Evasive reply	xxviii
Dissatisfied with Act of 1786—Two Quaker Grand Jurymen fined	xl, xli
Quee, Seth, Commissioner to receive oaths of allegiance	xxvi
Rankin, James, attainted	xxiii
Rawlings, Captain Thomas, a Tory, ordered to leave Pennsylvania	xxxii
Richards, John, Commissioner to receive oaths of allegiance	xxvi
Roberdeau, Daniel, elected Brigadier-General	xiii
Roberts, George, arrested	xxi
Roberts, Hugh, arrested	xxi
Ross, George, Vice President Convention to form State Constitution	xiv
Salomon, Haym, of Jewish Congregation, protests against religious test	xxxii
Seixas, Ger, Rabbi of Jewish Synagogue, protests against religious test	xxxii
Shee, Lieut. Col John, Chairman of a Meeting against Tories, 1783	xxx
Secretary of another meeting	xxxi
Shoemaker, Samuel, arrested	xxi
Attainted	xxiii
Sitgreaves, William, begs pardon for exceeding regulation price of coffee	ix
Smith, Jonathan B., Secretary State Conference	xix
Commissioner to receive oaths of allegiance	xxvi
Smith, Rev. William, arrested	xxi
Smith, William, (broker,) arrested	xxi
Smith, William Drewett, arrested	xxi
Stedman, Alexander, arrested	xxi
Stedman, Charles, Jr., arrested	xxi
Test, Religious, adopted by Conference of Associators	xiv
Tories—A powerful minority in Pennsylvania	vi
Kept down by committees	vii
Recantations by	vii, viii, ix, x
Favor the continuance of the Assembly of 1775-6, as State Government	xiii
Insolence of—Test and oath of allegiance demanded in consequence	xvii
Several Tories arrested by order of Congress—Sent to Winchester, Virginia	xx, xxi
Certain privileges guaranteed by Provisional Treaty with Great Britain—Resolves of the Philadelphia militia against them—Meetings concerning the same	xxx

	PAGE
Tories—Resolution that certain Tories shall withdraw from Philadelphia in ten days	xxxi
Tories—See "Quakers," "Allegiance," "Associators," "Assembly."	
Vernon, Nathaniel, attainted	xxiii
Warder, Jeremiah, arrested	xxi
Wayne, Gen. Anthony, favors the petitions of Non-jurors for repeal of test laws, 1785	xxxvi
The result	xxxvii
Wickersham, Amos, his recantation	vii
Wharton, Thomas, Senr., arrested	xxi
Young, James, Commissioner to take oaths of allegiance	xxvi
Young, Thomas, a Tory, ordered to leave Pennsylvania	xxxii

INDEX OF NAMES.

NOTE.—*The names in italics are those who did not subscribe to the Oath, but who are mentioned incidentally.*

Name	PAGE	Name	PAGE
Ackley, Daniel	71	Armet, John	48
Adams, Christopher	59	Armitage, John	42
Adams, John	28	Armitage, Shewbart	53
Adams, Jonathan	24	Armstrong, Christopher	81
Adams, Thomas	28	Armstrong, James	16
Adcock, (Justice)	30	Armstrong, John	13
Ahl, Johan Peter	64	Armstrong, William	52
Airhott, Johan Michael	77	Arndt, Jacob	2
Aitken, Andrew	26	*Arnold, (Gen.)*	79
Akely, Abraham	12	Ash, Caleb	36
Albers, Andrew	95	Ash, Jacob	38
Albert, George Adam	81	Ashton, William	54
Albert, Heinrich	85	Ashworth, Joseph	105
Albertson, Thomas	115	Assmus, John	88
Alborn, Imanuel Jacob	48	Atchison, William	72
Albrecht, William	4	Atkinson, John	85
Albright, Jacob	6	Attkinson, George	3
Alenby, James	67	Avered, Seth	26
Alexander, Alexander	58		
Alexander, William	58	Backius, Godfrey	12
Allen, Edward	100	Baes, John	111
Allen, John	22	Baker, Christopher	4, 36
Allen, John	40	Baker, Jacob	19, 41
Allenspacher, Joseph	99	Baker, Johannes Hilarius	42
Alston, Joseph	91	Baker, John	26
Altemus, Leonard	114	Baker, Samuel	5
Ames, James	98	Baker, Samuel	20
Amos, Jacob	4	Baker, William	14
Amos, Jacob	5	Ballam, Matthew	24, 89
Amos, John	4	Bandonino, William	117
Anderson, George	84	Bankson, Jacob	14
Anderson, James	95	Bankson, William	30
Anderson, James	114	Barber, William	67
Anderson, John	14	Barclay, Alexander	14
Anderson, John	113	Barclay, John	11
Anderson, Joseph	31	Bardeek, Georg	59
Anderson, William	118	Bare, Jacob,	18
Andrews, John	4	Bare, John,	16
Andrews, Peter	117	Bare, John,	18
Anton, Gottlieb	83	Barge, Jacob	58
Antony, Manuel	116	Barnes, Cornelius	41
Appel, Daniel	21	Barnhill, Daniel	63
Apt, George	12	Barnhill, John, Junr.	56

INDEX OF NAMES.

Name	PAGE
Barns, Arthur	78
Barns, Cornelius	73
Barns, Daniel	66
Barns, Maurice	88
Barns, William	37
Barr, Jacob	42
Barriere, Peter	99
Bass, Robert	17, 36
Bastian, Wilhelm	43
Bates, George	36
Batley, Thomas	91
Baumgart, Jacob	96
Baynton, Peter	58, 107
Beackley, Christian	8
Beaks, John	12
Beale, William	43
Bealer, David	56
Bealert, Jacob	37
Becher, Jacob	4
Bechtel, Georg	10
Beck, John	17
Beck, Thomas	12, 69
Beck, Thomas	36
Beckley, Daniel	69
Beckman, Johan Conrad	64
Bedford, Gunning	8, 38
Bedford, Joseph	19
Bedford, Peter	19
Beech, Edmond, Junr.	46
Beekman, Gerard William	42
Bell, George	8
Bell, James	69
Bell, John	5
Bell, Robert	20, 42
Bell, Thomas	27, 96
Bell, William	23
Bemé, Christian Gottlieb	100
Bender, Daniel	78
Bender, George	98
Benezet, Daniel	16
Benner, Martin	3
Bensted, Alexander	28
Bentley, Felix	46
Bentley, John	96
Berry, William	85
Berwick, James	105
Beyer, Carl	92
Biddle, Marks John	111
Biddle, William M.	111
Bidgood, Joseph	93
Bigony, John	6
Bigony, Joseph	6
Baron v. Bilow, Carl Ludewig	66

Name	PAGE
Bishop, Johann	77
Bitters, Charles	57
Black, John	93
Blackie, Robt.	116
Blain, John	86
Blaine, Ephraim	28
Blake, William	75
Blatterman, Henry	78
Blatzer, Charles	61
Bleakly, Archibald	99
Bleijer, Peter	90
Bloss, Friederich	87
Blunt, Stephen	20
Blutzer, Carl	14
Boatman, Philip	66
Bogen, (Doctr.)	96
Boinod, Daniel	101
Boland, Daniel	92
Bolter, Joseph	48
Bond, George	23
Booker, Thomas	51, 66
Boos, Charles Daniel	76
Bornman, Valentine	90
Bost, Jacob	14
Boulter, Benjamin	13
Boulter, Joseph	59
Bourne, Thomas	6
Boutman, Philip	66
Bowen, James	91
Bower, Charles	2
Bower, Francis	47
Bower, Jacob	64
Boyer, Abraham	111
Boyl, James	88
Boyle, James	79
Boyle, Peter	13
Boys, Elias, Junr.	116
Bradford, William	24
Bradley, Cornelius	104
Brady, Samuel	27
Brand, Andrew	2, 36
Brearly, Robert	109
Brehnert, Thomas	111
Brethower, Cooper	47
Brian, George	40
Brice, John	27
Briggs, John	118
Brittin, John	10
Brodie, Alexander	68
Brooke, Matthew	104
Brookes, John	45
Brown, Ephraim	110
Brown, Johann Conrad	5

INDEX OF NAMES.

Name	PAGE
Brown, John	37
Brown, John	76
Brown, Samuel Montgomery	71
Brown, William	57
Brown, William	103
Brown, William Montgomery	74
Bruce, Peter	77
Bruner, Georg	79
Brunot, Felix	99
Brunstrong, John	108
Brunton, James	90
Bruyn, Jan Christian	100
Bryan, George	2
Bryan, Guy	101
Bryan, John	19
Bryarly, John	26
Bryce, John	27
Buchanan, Eccles	108
Buchholtz, Valentin	82
Budden, William	13
Bulkely, Joseph	64
Buntin, Robert	112
Burgoyne, Gen.	90
Burkhard, Frederick	109
Burklae, Jacob	41
Burly, Christopher	63
Burn, Joshua	62
Burnes, John	36
Burnhouse, George	85
Burrage, John	93
Bush, Christian	75
Byron, Joshua	105
Cailleau, Peter L.	113
Cain, Michael	69
Calb, Jacob	72
Calbanan, John	51
Caldwell, James	16
Campbell, John	52
Campbell, John	100
Campbell, Kenneth	91
Caner, Michael	51
Cannan, Thomas	5
CAREY, MATTHEW	30
Carlin, Jonathan	89
Carlisle, Henry	97
Carlton, ——	90
Carns, John, Junr.	18
Carothers, John	116
Carr, Benjamin	71
Carr, James	18
Carradine, Thomas	20
Carrick, Jacob	36
Carrin, John	107
Carroll, James	97
Carstairs, Thomas	99
Carter, Thomas	9
Cartwright, Edward	14
Caruthers, James	12
Casey, Samuel	88
Casper, Martin	86
Cassellman, Wilhelm	86
Caster, Jacob	7
Causten, Isaac	13
Cavanaugh, Edward	41
Cavenough, William	101
Cecil, Charles	38
Chain, William	7
Chandler, George	3, 37
Channell, Samuel	56
Channell, Thomas	63
Chapman, Benjamin, Junr.	53
Chevilier, Christian	11
Child, John	104
Christ, Martin	65, 76
Christian, Frederick	70
Christy, James	5
Chrystie, James	27
Chrystler, Jacob	10
Clackner, George	20
Clampffer, Adam	36
Clarck, Gustav	86
Clark, Christopher	69
Clark, David	112
Clark, Michael	47
Clark, Thomas	103
Clark, William	42
Clark, William	55
Clauzer, Philip	9
Clay, Jonathan	14
Claypoole, George	18, 27, 33
Claypoole, James	4, 22
Clazer, John	51
Cleigner, Casper	51
Clinton, Church	109
Coates, John	43
Coats, Isaac	104
Coats, Thomas	118
Cochran, William	4
Codd, William	71
Coffin, Elijah	33
Coffman, John	37
Coffman, John	94
Colewater, Philip	30
Colflesh, Heinrich	17
Colflesh, Mathias	17

R.

INDEX OF NAMES.

Name	PAGE	Name	PAGE
Collins, James	72	Croghan, George	36
Collins, John	11	Croker, Ambrose	11
Collins, William	107	Crook, John	35
Collom, William	16	Crook, John	52
Colson, Francis	66	Crook, Joseph	87
Colvin, Hugh	9	Crotty, David	14
Comegys, Cornelius	58	Crowden, John	1
Connell, George	41	*Crugh, John*	41
Connell, William	86	Cubler, Jacob	103
Connelly, Patrick	106	Cullman, Adam	77
Conner, John	5	Culnan, John	93
Conner, Paul	8	Cumfort, Francis	103
Connor, John	65	Cummings, John	37
Connor, Michael	25	Cunningham, William	118
Conrad, Jacob, Junr.	3	Curry, Robert	7
Conrad, Philip	38		
Conrod, Jacob	6	Dallas, A. J.	96
Conrod, Jacob	36	Dallas, Stewart George	96
Conyngham, Frederick	118	Daller, Michael	83
Cook, George	14	Dame, Christian	52
Cook, John	22	Damm, Andrew	6
Cooper, Annanius	106	Daniel, John	5
Cope, Mathias	48	Daniel, John	10
Copple, John	11	Darrach, John	19
Corbright, John	10	Darragh, Charles	25
Cornman, John	38	Davan, John	98
Cornish, Robert	15	David, John	40
Corse, John	19	Davidson, James	70
Cottman, John	42	Davidson, Robert	41
Cottringer, James	21	Davidson, William	47
Coulthurst, Matthew	91	Davies, David	8
Course, Isaac	11	Davies, William	6
Coulty, Samuel	54	Davis, Isaac	69
Cove, John	88	Davis, James	93
Cowan, James	113	Davis, James	9, 39
Cowell, John	25	Davis, John	39
Cowie, Andrew	94	Davis, John	106
Cox, Jacob	29	Davis, Jonathan	95
Cox, Thomas	89	Davis, Joseph	111
Craig, Daniel	61	Davis, Peter	78
Craig, Thomas	46, 102	*Davis, (Justice)*	45
Craig, Thomas	118	Daw, John	21
Crain, Robt.	20	Day, Andrew	56
Crass, Peter	38	Deak, Thomas	60
Crawford, Charles	96	Deal, John	13
Crawford, John	112	Deamand, George	103
Crawford, Joseph	30	Dean, Conrod	90
Crawford, Samuel	10	Decoster, Charles	71
Cress, Henry	47	De Cressy, Maximilian L. A.	100
Cress, Johannes	98	De Dcke, Carl	105
Crimshew, John David	70	Deering, Nicholas	73
Crispin, Peter	3	Defrancquen, Philip	111
Crispin, Samuel	54	Degenhart, Johann George	53

INDEX OF NAMES.

Name	PAGE
De Grofey, Charles	117
De Haven, Peter	53
Deimling, Frederick	88
De la Croix, Joseph	99
Delaney, George	17
Delaney, James	96
Delaplaine, James	19
Dellap, Williams	19
Delonguay, Francis Moussu	94
Demd, Henry	85
Dempsey, Barnaby	4
Denci, (Justice)	110
Denny, David	92
Denny, Richard	109
Derry, George	89
Desantee, Lewis	71
Deshong, Friederich	39
Detterline, Henry	104
Dewees, William	68
Dewers, Henry	76
Dewetter, Conrad	37
Dexter, James	43
Dey, Cornelius	74
Diamond, John	16, 39
Dickens, Edward	12
Dickinson, Cadr.	59
Dickinson, Maurice	110
Dickson, Thomas	52
Dieffenbach, Christopher Frederick	69
Dill, Balthazar	82
Dill, Nicholaus	103
Dishong, Christian	50
Ditrich, Michael	45
Dolby, Joseph	70
Domiller, William	43
Donaldson & Co.	75
Donnelly, Francis	23
Donnelly, Terence	15
Donohue, John	29
Donovan, William	107
Dorey, Peter Victor	104
Douglass, E.	109
Douglass, John	11
Douglass, John	88
Douglas, William	21
Dover, Frederick	102
Dow, Benjamin	89
Dowling, Kerence	65
Downey, William	92
Downing, Nicholas	93
Downs, Robert	71
Doz, Andrew	3, 52
Draper, Jonathan	3, 38
Ducomb, Vincent	112
Dudengöss, Ludwig	82
Due, William	21
Duffus, Andrew	113
Duffy, James	23
Duffy, Patrick	25
Duguid, John, Junr.	92
Dumfield, John	9
Dun, John	113
Dunbar, James	82
Dunhower, George	7
Dunlap, James	3
Dunn, Isaac B.	28
Dunn, Philip	115
Dunton, William	5
Durie, John	78
Durling, Joseph	5
Du Simitiere, P. E.	9
Duy, Frederick	54
Ebalt, John	118
Ebert, Johannes	97
Eckhart, William	49
Eckelman, Conrad	60
Eckstein, Jacob	109
Eddleston, Lawrence	83
Eddy, George	92
Edeling, Johann Valtin	82
Egen, Leonard	6
Eggers, Nicholas	68
Ehrenzeller, Jacob	49
Eikhart, Matthias	87
Elder, Joshua	59
Elliott, Christopher	7
Elliott, David	25
Elliott, Edward	18
Emory, Jabez	115
Endesruggern, Ernst	84
Engle, Benjamin	103
Ent, Theobald	40
Ermanberger, Friederich	53
Erringer, Jacob	3, 39
Esenbeck, William	80
Eshrick, George	81
Esling, Frederick	102
Esling, Nicholas	71
Esling, Paul	102
Evans, Caleb	101
Evans, David	101
Evans, Lewis	115
Evans, Samuel	39
Everhard, David	55, 101
Everhart, John	55

INDEX OF NAMES.

Name	Page
Everly, John	47
Facundas, Jacob	11
Fagan, Edmond	20
Fajon, John	7
Falkener, William	101
Falkenstein, Ludwig	39
Farnsworth, James	20
Fecundas, William	57
Feel, Rudolph	64
Fegal, John	18
Ferguson, Ephraim	107
Ferguson, Hugh	13
Ferguson, William	117
Fesmore, John	23
Fians, William	7
Field, Peter	102
Finley, Francis	36
Finley, James	28
Fineton, John	112
Fisher, Andreas	9
Fisher, George	5
Fisher, Johannes	99
Fisher, John	56
Fisler, Jacob	5, 36
Fite, Andrew	6
Fitzgerald, Thomas	43
Fitzpatrick, John	75
Fitzsimons, John	117
Fleeson, Plunket	35, 45, 62
Fleeson, Thomas	40
Fleisher, Casper	12
Floak, Justice	96
Flounders, Edward	48
Folk, Matthew	11
Folt, Daniel	21
Folwell, William	20
Footman, Peter	17
Ford, Christopher	114
Ford, John	43
Forgey, William	115
Forst, Abraham	68
Forster, C. Martin	52
Forster, John	52
Forsyth, George	18
Fourage, Stephen	61
Fox, George	36
Fox, John	74
Fox, John George, Senr.	6
Fox, Justinian	50
Fox, Michael	14
Foy, Matthew	43
Fraley, John	54
Francis, Jacob	84
Francis, Tench	18
Francis, Thomas	43
Frank, Isaac	99
Frank, Jacob	17
Franses, Peter	85
Fraser, Samuel	95
Frazer, John	22
Frichman, Johann Heinrich	86
Friedelbach, Johann	91
Friederich, Wilhelm	9
Fritenheiler, Adam	90
Fry, John	4
Fryhoffer, John	18
Fryhoffer, Wollery	18
Fuller, Benjamin	2
Fullerton, Robert	50, 59
Fullerton, William	5
Gaa, Gilbert	110
Gaillard, Alexander	101
Galvan, John	110
Gamble, James	63
Gameber, Michael	57
Garand, Jacob	102
Garanger, Lewis	105
Gardenok, Powel Adam	69
Gardette, James	110
Gardner, John	3
Garhart, Daniel	30
Garman, William	77
Garrett, Adam	14
Garrett, Conrad	111
Gebheart, Georg	54
Gebler, Godfred	66
Gehring, Michael	79
Geiss, Everhart	2
Geisse, Francis	11
Gentle, James	73
George, Andrew	50
George, George	51
George, John	50
George, John, Junr.	50
Gibbons, Henry	10
Gibbs, Josiah W.	107
Giessler, Johannes	83
Gilbert, Jacob	2
Gilbert, Jacob, Junr.	2
Gilchrist, Adam	22
Gilchrist, James	26
Gilchrist, John	71
Gillingham, James	62
Gill, Josiah	8

INDEX OF NAMES.

Name	Page	Name	Page
Gitts, Michael	51	Grisler, Frederick	13
Glick, Johann	83	Grobey, Johann	97
Glisson, William	51	Groff, Adam	40
Gloeding, Abraham	47	Grosse, (Doctr.)	96
Glyn, Patrick	116	Grotz, George	8
Godfrey, William E.	18	Grover, John	17
Godshall, John	109	Grubb, John Herbert	73
Goette, Israel	98	Grunwold, Frederick	78
Goggin, Williams	58	*Guier, Adam*	101
Goldschmitt, Caspar	77	Guier, John	101
Gominger, Jacob	19	Guiney, William	41
Goodman, Conrod	18, 39	Guinop, William	54
Goodman, John	7	Gusse, Francis	58, 59
Goodman, John	111	Guy, John	12
Gorgas, Benjamin	5	Guy, Richard	12
Gorgas, John	5		
Gosner, Casper	58	Haas, Jacob	7
Gosner, Daniel	50	Hager, Martin	95
Gotlib, Conrad	87	Hague, Elsha	117
Gotthart, Johann Conrad	35	Hain, John	57
Govett, James	40	Haines, Michael	116
Grab, Peter	49	Halburtat, John	36
Graff, Jacob	4	Hale, Thomas	9
Graham, Matthew	107	Hall, James	35
Graham, William	23, 42	Hall, James	101
-Graner, Frederic	91	Hall, Parry	96
Grant, Alexander	116	Hall, Reuben	7
Grant, Henry	93	Hall, Richard	12
Grant, Isaac	7	Hall, Thomas	36
Grant, Peter	59	Hall, Walter	15
Gratz, Michael	52	Hallam, Lewis	98
Gravel, John	43	Halling, Solomon	49
Gray, Joseph	70	Hambright, John	7
Gray, William	25	Hamel, James	25
Gray, William	67	Hamilton, Andrew	18, 48
Gray, William	70	Hamilton, Henry	94
Greble, John	48	Hamilton, John	73
Green, Nathaniel	4	Hamilton, John	88
Green, Peter	13	Hamilton, John	99
Green, Gen.	20	Hamilton, W.	38
Greenway, William	7	Hammer, Henry	92
Greenwood, Alexander	60	Hankel, Conrad	76
Greer, Charles	51	Hankel, Jacob	41
Greer, George	118	Hans, Conrad	59
Greer, Henry	99	Hansell, David	15
Gregg, Robert	29	Hansell, William	10
Greswold, Thomas	17	Hansil, Peter David	6
Greve, Henry	28	Hansman, Christian	36
Griffith, Cadwalader	117	Harar, Daniel	43
Griffith, Evan	42	Harbeson, Benjamin, Junr.	115
Griffith, William	12	Hargis, Abraham	22
Grim, Nicholas	13	Harkness, Samuel	109
Grimes, John	71	Harly, George	60

	PAGE		PAGE
Harma, Joseph	27	Hickey, Timothy	75
Harman, George	111	Hiffernan, John	54
Harman, George	111	Hillborn, Joseph	16, 44
Harman, Jacob	1	Hillborn, Miles	3
Harper, John	86	Hines, Thomas	83
Harraway, John	6	Hiney, George	12
Harris, Henry	31, 85	Hinkle, Nicholas	22
Harris, James	15, 38	Hinton, George	74
Harrison, Joseph	100	Hitchings, William Vaughan	63
Harrison, William P.	112	Hitner, Frederick	5
Hart, Christopher	40	Hodge, Andrew, Junr.	15
Hart, George	10	*Hodgkinson, Bethenah*	70
Hart, Henry	10	Hodgson, Alvery	8
Hart, Joseph	2	Hodgson, Joseph	114
Hartlan, Johan	79	Hoffer, Philip	51
Harvey, Joseph	10	Hoffner, George	26
Hasig, Valentine	10	Hoffstedler, John	14
Haussman, John D.	99	Hoggen, James	102
Havesstrick, Jonas	87	Hohnerson, Matthias	91
Hay, John	11	Holeget, Matthew	6
Hayes, Isaac	53	Holegit, John	5
Hazen, ——	26	Holland, Benjamin	19
Hazleton, Albright	60	Hollinshead, William	4
Hazleton, Josiah	13	Holmes, Abraham	8
Hazlewanger, Lewis	4	Holsten, Frederick	7
Hazlewood, John, Junr.	28	Holsten, Matthias	7
Hazley, Charles	82	Holsten, Peter	8
Healy, William	105	Honaker, Joseph	100
Heatly, Charles	76	Honeycomb, Joseph	48
Heaton, Jonathan	47	Honeyman, Samuel	59
Heinrichs, Philip	55	Honeyman, William	29
Heizer, Henry	82	Hood, Thomas	107
Heffernan, John	17	Hoofman, James	116
Heller, Johannes	40	Hook, George	68
Heller, Joseph	24	Hook, William	82
Helm, John	50	Hooker, Thomas	87
Hembel, Samuel	22	Hooper, Matthew	48
Henderich, Johan Martin	96	Horn, John	9
Henderson, John	8, 44	Horner, James	2
Henderson, William	23	Hossman, Stokely	7
Henry, John	73	Houlgate, Cornelius	6
Herfford, George	76	Houshold, Sebastian	9
Herron, James G.	26	Howell, Abraham	27
Hess, George	12	Howell, David	89
Hess, John	117	Howell, Richard	99
Hess, Nicholas	117	Huber, Georg	72
Hetherington, John	60	Hubley, Adam	1
Hettmannkerger, Frantz Wilhelm	57	*Hubley, (Justice)*	105
Heyl, George	49	Huckel, William	91
Heyl, John	40	Hudson, Henry	70
Heyneman, Heynrich	82	Hudson, James	15
Heysham, Robert	16	Hudson, John	110
Hibberd, Joseph	17, 48	Hufty, Simon	42

INDEX OF NAMES.

Name	PAGE
Huggins, George	89
Hugh, William	106
Hughes, John	66
Hull, (Justice)	47
Humphreys, Benjamin	40
Humphreys, James	13
Humphreys, Samuel	53
Humphreys, Thomas	18
Hunn, John	26
Hunt, Gilbert	90
Hunt, Richard	38
Hunt, William	57
Hunter, Charles	98
Huntheimer, Tictus	87
Hurley, Thomas	114
Hurry, Arthur	15
Hurst, James	73
Huston, Edward	61
Hutman, Peter	11
Huvort, Loedwick	98
Hyneman, Frederick	115
Hyneman, Henry	11
Hynes, Brian	71
Hysmmingle, Nicholas	12
Ilgen, Lewis	80
Ingiez, Jerom	49
Inglis, George	74
Ioane, Marcus	68
Ironning, George	11
Irwin, Robert	6
Irwin, Thomas	38
Isaac, Charles	70
Isinhoot, Andrew	13
Israel, Israel	110
Jackson, James	79
Jackson, John M.	20
Jackson, Thomas	85
Jackson, William	16
Jacobs, Nicholas	3
Jagger, Abraham	88
James, Benjamin	113
Jamison, John	26
Janus, George	8
Jarvis, Jacob	76
Jeffery, William	19
Jervis, John	67
Jewell, Robert	2
Johner, Georg	66
Johnson, John	108
Johnston, James	97
Johnston, John	22
Johnston, Robert	113
Jonasson, Neels	7
Jones, David	1
Jones, Francis	19, 42
Jones, George Buch	90
Jones, Israel	17
Jones, Jesse	16
Jones, John	24
Jones, Joshua	17
JONES, PAUL	28
Jones, William	5
Jones, William	16, 36
Jordan, Joseph	116
Jude, Frederick	104
Junkin, Samuel	42
Jutter, Johann Christopher	35
Kaje, Augustus	80
Katz, Heinrich	53
Katz, Henry	7
Kauch, Christian	81
Kaworth, John	25
Keating, Luke	35
Keavort, Christian	84
Keble, John	4
Keeling, John Hignet	52
Keen, Joseph	103
Keene, L.	28
Keichler, John	38
Keidel, George	78
Keisler, Jacob	9
Keller, Conrad	69
Kelley, James	50
Kelly, John	4
Kelly, William	94
Kelsey, Joshua	89
Kemble, Peter	76
Kemble, William	43
Kemmel, Peter	90
Kendall, Joseph	5
Kenedy, John	75
Kennedy, Robert	22
Kephard, Coron	60
Keram, Edward	4
Kerlin, John, Junr.	51
Kesler, Henry	105
Kessler, Leonard	20
Keys, John	13
Keyser, John	75
Kidd, William	3
Killamer, Hance	84
Kimhel, Heinrich	52
Kinder, Gottlieb	100

INDEX OF NAMES.

Name	PAGE
King, Abraham	75
King, Isaac	73
King, James	106
Kingsfield, Wendell	4
Kinkead, James	50
Kinnard, Jacob	41
Kinnear, James	17
Kinsel, John	117
Kintzing, Abraham, Junr.	107
Kipp, Andreas	83
Kirk, Anthony	47
Kirk, James	21
Kirkbride, (Col.)	53
Kirkhoff, Christian	12
Kirwan, Nicholas	73
Klein, Johan	79
Klein, Philip	29
Knight, Charles	16
Knoepler, George	67
Knoll, Ludwick	18, 39
Knowles, John	83
Knox, Francis	29
Knox, Hugh	20
Knox, Mathew	55
Koehler, Bernhard	79
Koehler, John Adam	59
Koehmle, John	51
Köhr, Philip	82
Kook, John	35
Kooper, Georg	106
Kooper, George	46
Korloder, Friederich	88
Korn, Gabriel	42
Koy, William	79
Krafst, Michael	61
Kreaning, Francis	76
Kresson, Joseph	114
Kromer, Leonard	2
Krop, Jean	100
Kubler, Martin	108
Kugler, Christopher	28
Kunze, John C.	36
Kurtz, George	36
Kurtz, Peter	17
Lackrum, John	108
Lahn, Jacob	98
Lake, Richard	105
Lake, Thomas	23
Lake, Capt. Thomas	23
Lake, William	41
Lambeth, Joseph	109
Landerken, Patrick	74
Lang, Thomas	112
Langdale, Samuel	3, 39
Langrall, Levin	24
Laodie, John Claude	95
Larrison, George	72
Latch, Jacob	36
Latch, Rudolph	8
Lauer, Philip	27
Laughlin, Jacob	7
Lavisyler, Thomas	28
Lawrence, John	51
Lawrence, William	3
Lawrence, William	56
Lawson, John	15
Lawyer, Christian	18
Laycock, John	94
Leaman, Joseph	3
Lear, John	42
Lear, John L.	65
Leavering, Benjamin	4
Lechler, Adam	58
Ledra, Joseph	20
Leech, Isaac	20
Leech, Peter	80
Leech, Robert	12
Lehré, Jacob	50
Leib, Michael	17
Leitshok, Conrad	87
Lemaigre, Pierre	64
Lemaire, Jean Baptiste	113
Lemau, Andrew	9
Lennerd, John	45
Lentz, Heinrich	9
Lentz, Henry	101
Lentz, John	101
Leonard, Joseph	40
Lesh, Zachariah	97
Letchworth, John	104
Letts, Michael	15
Levering, Abraham	2
Levering, Jacob	8
Levering, William	102
Levering, William	102
Levy, Eleazer	18
Lewis, John	79
Lewis, Joseph	54
Lewis, Pearce	12
Liberstin, Felix	54
Ligaux, Peter	112
Light, James	56
Light, Peter	16
Lincoln, James	64
Linnard, William	65

INDEX OF NAMES.

Name	Page	Name	Page
Linniberger, John	53	Macpherson, William	91
Lint, Frederick	53	Maffett, Joseph	108
Linton, John	55	Maher, Martin	97
Lippee, John	11	Makemson, George	47
Lipsey, Henry	30	Malone, John	10
Lisle, Joseph	41	Malone, Peter	67
Litchenham, Jacob	39	Mandry, Richard	81
Llewelyn, John	19	Maner, Julius	117
Llewelyn, Morriss	19	Mansai, Nicola	113
Loardan, Charles	11	Marcer, Benjamin James	72
Lockhart, William	103	Marcus, Johannes	70
Lockwood, James	29	Markoe, Peter	99
Lodge, John	5	Marks, Levy	3
Logan, Charles	15	Marsan, John	97
Loge, John	26	Marshal, Anthony	71
Lohman, William	13	Martin, Hugh	26
Lohra, John	20	Martin, John	46
Long, John	43	Martin, William	27
Loomsbach, Johannes	76	Mathes, John	49
Lorden, Charles	60	Mathias, Joseph	19
Lorden, George	43	MATLACK, TIMOTHY	? 73
Lotie, Laurence	117	Matlack, William	3, 36
Loughlin, (Squire)	107	Mattson, Israel	63
Louriette, Zachariah	105	Matzinger, George	42
Loving, Casper	64	Matzinger, John	7
Lowden, Jacob	111	Maur, Jacob	53
Lownes, Joseph	19	May, John	89
Lowrey, Samuel	108	Mayer, George	26
Loxly, Benjamin, Junr.	1	*Mayer, Jacob*	26
Lubrer, Adrien Joseph	113	Mayer, Johannes	72
Lucas, James	11	*Mayland, (Col.)*	66
Ludgate, Richard	15, 53	Maynard, Joseph	73
Lumsden, Robert	116	Maysey, Thomas	110
Lutch, Jacob	6	McAlestor, John	18
Luther, Conrod	92	McAnally, Henry	30
Luts, Christian	66	McCall, David	114
Lutz, Conrad	4	McCarter, Charles	25
Lutz, Johann	83	McCarter, Daniel	95
Luy, Hoyman	46	McCartney, John	10
Luzer, John Andrew	92	McCarty, Marks	89
Lynch, John	111	McCary, Daniel	63
Lynch, John Patrick	68	McCausland, Marcus	71
Lynn, Jeremiah	19	McCausland, Robert	74
Lyon, Philip	91	McClarey, Archibald	23
Lyon, Samuel	3	McClatchie, William	50
Lyons, James	63	McClenney, Thomas	76
Lytle, Andrew	26	McClentick, Matthew	29
		McCollin, Andrew	59
Maag, Jacob	14	McCotter, James	6
Mackay, James	111	McCrea, Fergus	77
Mackenzie, William	19	McCulley, Thomas	104
Macky, John	2	McCulloh, John	6
Macombe, James	96	McDermott, William	109

S

INDEX OF NAMES.

Name	Page	Name	Page
McDonald, Alexander	108	Metzinger, Michael	3
McDonald, Donald	104	Mevins, Henry	71
McDonald, William	81	Meyer, Joseph	9
McDonnell, Edward	40	Meyland, Siméon	65
McDowell, Thomas	4, 49	Middlehauser, Friederich	80
McElroy, Benjamin	110	Midwinter, John	89
McElvain, William	38	Miers, Christopher	50
McFarland, Kennedy	92	Miller, Andrew	23
McFarlane, John	14	Miller, Benjamin	48
McGee, Henry	8	Miller, Caspar	83
McGill, James	1	Miller, Christopher	46
McGouen, John	93	Miller, Henry	95
McGregor, John	79	Miller, Jacob	102
McGregor, Richard	78	Miller, Johan Georg	36
McGuire, Matthew	25	Miller, John	15
McIlench, John	30	Miller, John	84
McIntire, Andrew	12	Miller, John	93
McIntire, Thomas	28	Miller, Magnus	95
McIntosh, Donald	55	Miller, Martin	7
McIntosh, John	99	Miller, Nicholas	14
McKendrick, Archibald	39	Miller, Robert	15
McKennan, John	51	Miller, William	14
McKenzie, William Jackson	106	Miller, William	95
McKiernan, Charles	116	Miller, William	103
McKim, John	4	Mills, John	15
McKinsey, John	111	Mingle, John	117
McLean, Daniel	21	Mitchel, John	56
McLean, James	25	Mitchell, Hugh	10
McLean, Keneth	78	Mitchell, John	29
McMahon, Michael	88	Mits, John Conrad	104
McMichael, William	46	Molineux, Frederick	98
McMillen, James	77	Montgomery, Daniel	74
McMullen, James	80	Montgomery, Duncan	110
McMullen, Michael	20	Montgomery, James	23
McNachtane, John	74	Montgomery, William	31
McNair, John	14	Moore, Bartholomew	2
McSparran, William	9	Moore, George	65
McVeagh, Benjamin	56	Moore, George	106
Meade, George	97	Moore, Hugh	76
Mears, John	94	Moore, J.	27
Meayn, Ludwig	80	Moore, John	11
Mellen, Peter	41	Moore, John	75
Mellenberger, Peter	13	Moore, Philip	24
Mellor, Johann Xhart	64	Moore, Robert	41
Melvin, Robert	84	Moore, Robert K.	115
Mentges, Philip	27	Moore, William	37
Mentz, Jomel	94	Moore, William	43
Mercier, Joseph	104	*Moore, (Justice)*	60
Meridith, Charles	16	Morgan, John	51
Mervine, Andrew	4	Morgan, Thomas	17
Mesnard, Thomas	63	Morgan, Thomas	42
Metay, William	11	Morrell, Robert	27, 97
Metts, Adam	43	Morris, Evan	9

INDEX OF NAMES.

Name	PAGE
Morris, Luke, Junr.	21
Morris, Thomas A.	104
Morrison, Daniel	11
Morton, George	8
Morton, Israel	7
Moser, George	14
Moylan, Jasper Alexander	70
Moylan, John	70
Moyston, Edward	106
Muller, Christian	81
Müller, Johannes	55
Müller, Michael	15
Murdaugh, James	48
Murgatroyd, John	10
Murphy, Alexander	93
Murphy, Thomas	71
Murry, Jeremiah	74
Mussi, Joseph	114
Muster, John	83
Myers, Henry	84
Myrtelus, Adam	3
Naer, David	66
Nassau, John	96
Neffets, Edward	63
Neill, James	37
Nesbit, J. M.	2
Nevell, Thomas	6
Nevil, James	96
Newark, Thomas	73
Newel, David	116
Nice, John	59
Nice, Lewis	62
Nicholas, William	54
Nicol, Robert	112
Nicholson, John	113
Niemond, Johann	89
Nimmo, Alexander	104
Nixon, John	2
Nolbrow, William	15
Nouveller, Matthias	37
Norton, William	29
Nourse, Joseph	68
Nuff, Melchoir	40
Nugent, Edmond	18, 46
Nugent, James	65
O'Donnell, Patrick	75
Oellers, James	46
Ogden, John	24
Ogden, Joseph, Junr.	61, 64
Oill, Henry	92

Name	PAGE
Oliver, George	73
O'Neill, Alexander Louis	69
O'Neill, Thomas	106
Opperman, Adam	77
Ord, John	49
Organ, John	30
Orner, Michael	2
Osmos, Henry	91
Oswald, Eleazer	23
Oswald, Robert	113
Otenkerken, John	17
Ott, Peter	21
Otto, Francis	77
Otto, Johannes	83
Overly, John	38
Overstake, Christian	56
Owens, Patrick	25
Owens, William	115
Packer, James	40
Paisley, Robert	114
Paleske, Charles	105
Palmer, John	16, 46
Palmer, Joseph	18, 49
Palmer, Thomas	41
Pancoast, David	18
Panrert, Johann	64
Parker, Richard	106
Parkes, Joseph	45
Parkhill, Andrew	63
Parkhill, John	13
Parkmann, Johannes	77
Paschal, Benjamin	48
Paschall, Benjamin	2
Paschall, Benjamin	8
Paschall, Thomas	44
Patterson, John	35
Pattison, Robert	24
Patton, John	27
Patton, William	26
Paul, David	6
Paul, Jonathan	6
Peale, James	18
Pearson, Joshua	20
Peiss, George	53
Pelozi, Vicenzo Maria	100
Peltz, Philip	103
Pemberton, Handy	106
Pemberton, Joseph	46
Pendleton, Solomon	95
Penington, Daniel	110
Penrose, Isaac	19
Penrose, Samuel	17, 48

INDEX OF NAMES.

Name	Page	Name	Page
Perkins, William	66	Pugh, Henry	19
Perree, Nicholas	64	Pugh, William	36
Perret, Henry	13	*Pulaski, Count*	69
Perry, Richard	73		
Peterman, Christian	47	Quain, John	14
Peters, Garrett	26	Queerfort, Henry	90
Peters, Capt. John	58	Quest, Nicholas	54
Peters, Samuel	17	Quin, Jeremiah	57
Peters, William, Junr.	74	Quinlen, John	97
Pettit, Charles	23		
Pettit, Thomas	72	Rambo, Peter	16
Phelps, Matthew	22	Randall, Thomas	108
Phile, Charles	50	Ranganer, Jacob	79
Phile, John	23	Rasbotham, James	41
Phillips, John	100	Ratzner, George	18
Pierie, Martin	53	Read, George	76
Pigeon, Conrad	12	Read, James	2
Pigisson, John	95	Read, John	28
Pine, Lazarus	6	Read, Samuel	75
Pine, Robert E.	113	Rede, Zeman Thomas	98
Pinkerton, William	105	Reed, Christopher	58
Pinton, William	46	Reed, Francis	81
Pittman, Zacarius	85	REED, JOSEPH	2
Plack, Friederich	37	Rees, James	114
Plain, Felix	85	Reffert, Philip	6
Platt, Daniel	93	Reid, Christopher	44
Pleiney, John	70	*Reidezel, ——*	95
Plunket, Robert	42	Reiley, John, Junr.	41
Pollard, John	59	Reiley, Patrick	65
Pollock, Oliver	116	Reinbott, Christian Friederich	81
Pool, Edward	28	*Reinhard, Martin*	101
Porter, David	25	Reinhard, Peter	101
Porter, John	17	Reinhart, George	60
Porter, John	50	Remender, Peter	39
Pot, Mattis	60	Renno, Jacob	45
Poth, Adam, Junr.	57	Renshaw, Thomas	47
Poth, Johannes	57	Reshong, David	61
Powell, Anthony	81	Rey, Andrew	30
Powell, Lawrence	19	Rey, Jean Louis	15
Powell, Peter	55	Reynhart, Francis	77
Powell, William	13	Reynard, John	78
Power, Alexander	25	Rhea, John	27
Prescott, Roger	101	Rice, John	13
Presuhn, Heinrich	88	Rice, Joseph	25
Price, Edward	8	Rice, Nicholas	42
Price, Joseph	5	Richards, David	41
Price, Lewis	82	Richards, John, Junr.	112
Price, Rees	19, 37	Richards, William	7
Price, Richard	38	Richardson, William	109
Prichard, William	65	Richie, Edward	38
Pride, James	105	Richhowser, John	84
Pritchett, Rowland	67	Richman, Thomas	57
Pritner, Philip	17	Rickneal, Jacob	21

INDEX OF NAMES.

Name	PAGE
Riddle, David	19
Riddle, John	52
Ried, John	12
Riffets, Edward	55
Rigg, Robert	7
Righter, Daniel	2
Righter, John	2
Righter, John	2
Righter, John	35
Righter, Michael	2
Rinaldi, Charles	94
Ritgie, John	89
Ritiger, Johannes	9
RITTENHOUSE, DAVID	6, 99
Ritter, Charles	52
Robert, John	80
Roberts, Abraham	60
Roberts, Algernon	16
Roberts, James	110
Roberts, John	9, 42
Roberts, William	90
Robinett, Joseph	59
Robinson, James	86
Robinson, Richard	40
Robinson, William	36
Robinson, William	41
Robson, Robert	52
Rogers, Benjamin	101
Rogers, Isabella	70
Rogers, James	58
Ronals, James	77
Roney, James	107
Roof, John	99
Rose, Peter	8
Rose, William	7
Rosenberger, Godfrey	80
Ross, GEORGE	5
Ross, Hugh	39
Rossiter, Thomas, Junr.	48
Roth, Philip	5
Rothbottom, James	12
Rothmann, Johann	74
Roue, Thomas	41
Rouking, John	6
Roun, Conrad	110
Rowand, Jacob	8
Rudolph, Christian	49
Rudolph, George	114
Rudolph, Tobias	49
Rudolph, Wilhelm	96
Rue, Joseph	63
Rumble, Philip	3
Rumel, Georg	83
Rundleman, John	86
Rush, William	7
Rusk, William	10
Russegue, Timothy	79
Russell, Alexander	28
Russell, James	5, 40
Rutherford, John	13
Rutter, George	61
Ryan, Edward	80
Ryan, James	108
Ryan, Timothy	109
Ryan, Thomas	113
Sadler, John	102
Sainton, John	112
Saldrich, David	49
Sallier, Jacque	112
Saltar, Richard	4
Sample, Thomas	88
Sauder, Caspar	2
Saunders, William	39
Sautter, Johannes	87
Savage, Darby	39
Savett, Henry	14
Savidge, John	29
Saxton, Jared	50
Scheiler, Johann	80
Schin, Conrad	61
Schlosser, George	7
Schmidt, Caspar	94
Schmitt, Heinrich	69
Schmitt, Johannes	67
Schmitt, Valentin	76
Schmyser, Michael	53
Schneider, Christian	7
Schneider, George	14
Schneider, Johan	92
Schrack, Jacob	63
Schreiner, Jacob	6
Schunel, Baltus	80
Schwalbah, Henry	1
Schwallach, Heinrich	55
Scot, Robert	25
Scott, Thomas	2
Scott, William	94
Scravendyke, Peter	107
Scull, Benjamin	51
Scully, Barnaby	30
Sears, Lemuel	22
Seddon, Thomas	106
Seegez, Frederick	3
Seitz, John Adam	98
Seixas, Abraham	23

INDEX OF NAMES.

Name	Page	Name	Page
Sellers, David	50	Sink, George	12
Sellers, John, Junr.	107	Sinket, Daniel	89
Sellers, Joseph	4, 43	Sisson, Thomas	115
Sellers, Nn.	36	Sitzdorff, Wilhelm	94
Semple, Alexander	72	Skellorn, Richard	58
Semple, John	85	Sleigh, Christian	51
Serre, François	112	Sloan, William	10
Shagert, Bernhard	87	Smallwood, Peter	11
Shaller, Conrad	9	Smaltz, Heinrich	11
Shaper, John	14	Smith, Benjamin	23
Sharp, Andrew	5	Smith, Benjamin H.	114
Sharp, Jacob	5	Smith, Christopher	115
Sharswood, George	35	Smith, Daniel	95
Shaw, Daniel	12	Smith, George	115
Shaw, George	54	Smith, Hosea	21
Shaw, Patrick	29	Smith, Jacob	14
Shee, John	76	Smith, Jacob	62
Sheldon, Isaac	22	Smith, James	68
Shelvough, William	80	Smith, John	5
Shetler, Martin	95	Smith, John	28
Shetzline, Adam	66	Smith, John	37
Shields, John	94	*Smith, John*	60
Shiell, William, M D.	64	Smith, John Erdman	16
Shilling, Michael	13	Smith, Jonathan	13
Shisler, Godfrey	17, 53	Smith, Jonathan, Junr.	115
Shiver, Michael	54	Smith, Joseph	13
Shlotman, Alexander	95	Smith, Matthew	2
Shmid, Friederich	92	Smith, Michael	3
Sholtz, Martin Henry	95	Smith, Philip	24, 78
Shoster, Henry	8	Smith, Robert	97
Shove, John Albert	86	*Smith, Robert*	101
Shreiber, Jacob	86	Smith, Robert, Junr.	101
Shrive, Samuel	59	Smith, Samuel	64
Shriver, Joseph	4	Smith, Thomas	17
Shubert, Michael	5	Smith, Thomas	67
Shuchard, Peter	85	Smith, William	91
Shuder, Ludwick	60	Smith, William	110
Shughart, Johannes	96	Smith, William Austin	71
Shuman, Friederich	86	*Smithson, (Justice)*	20
Sibley, Jacob	24	Smock, Robert	26
Sibley, Rudolph	8, 38	Sneider, Benedict	60
Sicard, Stephen	100	Snelhart, John	65
Sickard, Georg David	16	Sneling, George	15
Sieman, Waldrop	78	Snyder, George	55
Sim, Robert	93	Snyder, John	114
Simes, Samuel	108	Solter, John	15
Simmons, Thomas	66	Soly, Alexander	18
Simon, Johan Barnard	67	Sothern, William	116
Simons, Stephen	46	Souder, Casper	47
Sims, Bartholomew	102	Sowersby, William	41
Simter, John	118	Soytder, Gotfred	80
Singelton, Richard	42	Spalter, John	85
Sink, Abraham	16	Sparks, Henry	73

INDEX OF NAMES. 143

Name	PAGE
Spede, John	20
Speel, George	66
Spence, Andrew	102
Spencer, Daniel	58
Spiegel, John	12
Spinks, James	39
Spitter, Christopher	108
Spooner, John	89
Spottswood, William	30
Stafford, John	24
Stagg, Benjamin	24
Stainbaugh, Johannes	96
Stanley, Michael	12
Stanley, Peter	102
Stanley, Valentine	102
Stanley, William	53
Stanton, Jonathan	63
Starke, John	10
Stear, George	81
Stedman, Charles	16
Steel, David	107
Steel, James	11
Steel, James	74
Steel, Thomas	24
Steel, Thomas	107
Steller, Adam	27
Steinmetz, John	18
Steinmires, Jacob	11
Stephnon, George	87
Stern, Samuel	11, 40
Sternbak, Henry	112
Stettenfield, Jacob	56
Stevens, James	105
Stewart, Alexander	97
Stewart, Charles	50
Stewart, James	114
Stewart, Robert	93
Stiles, John	26
Stiles, Joseph	8
Stiles, William	101
Stilwil, Charles	72
Stock, Philip	57
Stockham, George	36
Stokes, George	57
Stokes, James	75
Stoll, William	49
Stoltz, Conrad	46
Stone, John	1
Stoneman, John	53
Stoup, Vandel	84
Stout, Peter	9
Stoute, George	53
Stow, Charles	40

Name	PAGE
Stow, George	14
Stow, Lazarus	25
Stretch, Joseph	3
Stricker, John	25
Stroud, William	37
Stuart, John	51
Stull, Casper	60
Sturgis, James	10
Sturgis, Joseph	6
Summers, John	114
Summers, Samuel	91
Sutter, Peter	3
Sutton, John	60
Swain, William Nathaniel	105
Swartz, Philip	22
Swats, George	11
Swetzer, Conrad	59
Symington, Alexander	109
Syng, Philip	5
Taggart, David	52
Tawney, James	14
Taylor, Angus	118
Taylor, Jacob	109
Taylor, Ludwig	9
Taylor, Peter	6
Taylor, Richard	13, 57
Taylor, Robert	97
Taylor, Samuel	8
Taylor, Solomon	15
Teigh, Charles	67
Telman, John	67
Thaw, Benjamin	39
Thayer, Bartholomew	47
Thiell, Henry	10
Thomas, Absalom	107
Thomas, John	45
Thomas, Joseph	107
Thomas, Luke	74
Thomas, Peter	115
Thomas, William	91
Thompson, James	10
Thompson, James	35
Thompson, John	25
Thompson, Thomas	42
Thompson, William	98
Thomson, James Hampden	22
Thomson, William	41
Thorn, William	13
Thornhill, John, Junr.	11
Tibin, John, Junr.	3
Tilghman, Edward, Junr.	29
Till, George	13

INDEX OF NAMES.

Name	PAGE
Tilman, Christopher	84
Tiviman, Robert	88
Tobin, Edmond	50
Tod, Alexander	53
Tod, James	102
Todd, Charles	103
Todd, George	77
Tom, Samuel	36
Tomkins, John	47
Topliff, Richard	39
Tottie, Benjamin	49
Towers, Robert, Junr.	8
Town, Henry	108
Transo, John Jacob	56
Trempor, William	43
Tren, Jacob	20
Truckenmiller, Philip	3
Tudor, George	27
Tullon, Christian	110
Tullon, Godfrey	110
Turner, David	98
Tustin, William	43
Tybout, Andrew	3
Tyson, Matthias	19
Tyson, William	19
Umbright, Johan	15
Underwood, James	42
Van Beck, Christian	66
Vandegrift, Joshua	103
Van Eckhent, Charles	100
Vannost, John	43
Van Tassel, Justice	95
Van Vleck, Isaac	29
Vaughan, Thomas	4
Veder, John	98
Venia, Bastia	9
Vensell, George	87
Vestard, John	6
Vickers, Thomas	100
Vogel, Daniel	79
Wade, James	108
Wade, Thomas	51
Wagner, Ferdinand	90
Wahl, Johann Heinrich	84
Waine, John	13
Walker, George	16, 84
Wallace, John	67
Wallace, Richard	28
Wallace, Robert	27
Walravin, John	109
Walsh, James	49
Walter, Martin	38
Walters, Johannes	17
Walters, John	7
Warner, Isaac	39
Warner, Philip	40
Warner, William, Junr.	15
Warnick, Albert	98
Washington, (General)	70
Wasphael, Godfried	78
Wathens, Capt. Joseph	59
Watkings, Joseph	60
Watkins, William	6
Watson, Archibald	39
Watts, Robert	102
Watts, Thomas	37
Way, Andrew	10
Wayne, Abraham	55
Weaver, John	4
Weaver, John	17, 38
Weaver, Paul	94
Webb, Joseph	15
Weekes, Henry	97
Weiss, Matthias	51
Welch, Thomas	48
Wenemon, Philip	58
Werrebrouek, Andrew	113
West, James	49
Weston, William	58
Wetzel, Godfrey	66
Weyant, John	1
Weyland, Martin	28
Wharton, Carpenter	16
Wharton, Charles	17
Wharton, Isaac	17
Wharton, Lloyd	106
Whelan, Edward	27, 97
White, George	108
White, John	29, 50
White, John	53
White, Joseph	85
White, Peter	108
White, Silvester	75
White, Thomas	99
Whitehead, James	25
Whiteman, Caspar	19
Whiteman, John	13
Whiteman, John	54
Whitman, Jacob	46
Whittington, William	38
Widdos, Isaac	38
Wiear, James	90
Wiest, Heinrich	81

INDEX OF NAMES. 143

Name	PAGE	Name	PAGE
Spede, John	20	Stow, George	14
Speel, George	66	Stow, Lazarus	25
Spence, Andrew	102	Stretch, Joseph	3
Spencer, Daniel	58	Stricker, John	25
Spiegel, John	12	Stroud, William	37
Spinks, James	39	Stuart, John	51
Spitter, Christopher	108	Stull, Casper	60
Spooner, John	89	Sturgis, James	10
Spottswood, William	30	Sturgis, Joseph	6
Stafford, John	24	Summers, John	114
Stagg, Benjamin	24	Summers, Samuel	91
Stainbaugh, Johannes	96	Sutter, Peter	3
Stanley, Michael	12	Sutton, John	60
Stanley, Peter	102	Swain, William Nathaniel	105
Stanley, Valentine	102	Swartz, Philip	22
Stanley, William	53	Swats, George	11
Stanton, Jonathan	63	*Swetzer, Conrad*	59
Starke, John	10	Symington, Alexander	109
Stear, George	81	Syng, Philip	5
Stedman, Charles	16		
Steel, David	107	Taggart, David	52
Steel, James	11	Tawney, James	14
Steel, James	74	Taylor, Angus	118
Steel, Thomas	24	Taylor, Jacob	109
Steel, Thomas	107	Taylor, Ludwig	9
Steller, Adam	27	Taylor, Peter	6
Steinmetz, John	18	Taylor, Richard	13, 57
Steinmires, Jacob	11	Taylor, Robert	97
Stephnon, George	87	Taylor, Samuel	8
Stern, Samuel	11, 40	Taylor, Solomon	15
Sternbak, Henry	112	Teigh, Charles	67
Stettenfield, Jacob	56	Telman, John	67
Stevens, James	105	Thaw, Benjamin	39
Stewart, Alexander	97	Thayer, Bartholomew	47
Stewart, Charles	50	Thiell, Henry	10
Stewart, James	114	Thomas, Absalom	107
Stewart, Robert	93	Thomas, John	45
Stiles, John	26	Thomas, Joseph	107
Stiles, Joseph	8	Thomas, Luke	74
Stiles, William	101	Thomas, Peter	115
Stilwil, Charles	72	Thomas, William	91
Stock, Philip	57	Thompson, James	10
Stockham, George	36	Thompson, James	35
Stokes, George	57	Thompson, John	25
Stokes, James	75	Thompson, Thomas	42
Stoll, William	49	Thompson, William	98
Stoltz, Conrad	46	Thomson, James Hampden	22
Stone, John	1	Thomson, William	41
Stoneman, John	53	Thorn, William	13
Stoup, Vandel	84	Thornhill, John, Junr.	11
Stout, Peter	9	Tibin, John, Junr.	3
Stoute, George	53	Tilghman, Edward, Junr.	29
Stow, Charles	40	Till, George	13

INDEX OF NAMES.

Name	PAGE
Tilman, Christopher	84
Tiviman, Robert	88
Tobin, Edmond	50
Tod, Alexander	53
Tod, James	102
Todd, Charles	103
Todd, George	77
Tom, Samuel	36
Tomkins, John	47
Topliff, Richard	39
Tottie, Benjamin	49
Towers, Robert, Junr.	8
Town, Henry	108
Transo, John Jacob	56
Trempor, William	43
Tren, Jacob	20
Truckenmiller, Philip	3
Tudor, George	27
Tullon, Christian	110
Tullon, Godfrey	110
Turner, David	98
Tustin, William	43
Tybout, Andrew	3
Tyson, Matthias	19
Tyson, William	19
Umbright, Johan	15
Underwood, James	42
Van Beck, Christian	66
Vandegrift, Joshua	103
Van Eckhent, Charles	100
Vannost, John	43
Van Tassel, Justice	95
Van Vleck, Isaac	29
Vaughan, Thomas	4
Veder, John	98
Venia, Bastia	9
Vensell, George	87
Vestard, John	6
Vickers, Thomas	100
Vogel, Daniel	79
Wade, James	108
Wade, Thomas	51
Wagner, Ferdinand	90
Wahl, Johann Heinrich	84
Waine, John	13
Walker, George	16, 84
Wallace, John	67
Wallace, Richard	28
Wallace, Robert	27
Walravin, John	109

Name	PAGE
Walsh, James	49
Walter, Martin	38
Walters, Johannes	17
Walters, John	7
Warner, Isaac	39
Warner, Philip	40
Warner, William, Junr.	15
Warnick, Albert	98
Washington, (General)	70
Wasphael, Godfried	78
Wathens, Capt. Joseph	59
Watkings, Joseph	60
Watkins, William	6
Watson, Archibald	39
Watts, Robert	102
Watts, Thomas	37
Way, Andrew	10
Wayne, Abraham	55
Weaver, John	4
Weaver, John	17, 38
Weaver, Paul	94
Webb, Joseph	15
Weekes, Henry	97
Weiss, Matthias	51
Welch, Thomas	48
Wenemon, Philip	58
Werrebrouek, Andrew	113
West, James	49
Weston, William	58
Wetzel, Godfrey	66
Weyant, John	1
Weyland, Martin	28
Wharton, Carpenter	16
Wharton, Charles	17
Wharton, Isaac	17
Wharton, Lloyd	106
Whelan, Edward	27, 97
White, George	108
White, John	29, 50
White, John	53
White, Joseph	85
White, Peter	108
White, Silvester	75
White, Thomas	99
Whitehead, James	25
Whiteman, Caspar	19
Whiteman, John	13
Whiteman, John	54
Whitman, Jacob	46
Whittington, William	38
Widdos, Isaac	38
Wiear, James	90
Wiest, Heinrich	81

INDEX OF NAMES.

Name	PAGE	Name	PAGE
Williams, Bedford	23	Wright, William	10
Williams, Ennion	47	Wusman, Yorick	64
Williams, Humphrey	68	Wyant, John	12
Williams, James	103	Wynn, Pastorius	36
Williams, Jeremiah	56	Wynn, Thomas	116
Williams, John	18		
Williams, Thomas	82	Yard, James	117
Williams, William	25	Yerger, John	40
Williamson, James	99	Young, Andrew	60
Williamson, Joseph	40	Young, Edward	11
Willing, James	23	Young, George	9, 42
Willis, Seth	9	Young, John	10
Willson, John	109	Young, John	18
Willson, William	92	*Young, John*	66
Wilson, Robert	8	Young, Llewelyn	19
Wilson, William	52	Young, Philip	9
Wilson, William	72	Young, Philip	42
Winckel, Carsten	112	Young, Philip	103
Winckler, Frederick William	100	Young, Samuel	8
Winter, James	19	Young, William	104
Witherspoon, D.	23	Young, William	106
Wonderly, Jacob	115	*Young, (Justice)*	20, 48
Wood, George	37		
Wood, John	12	Zane, Jonathan	18
Wood, Joseph	49	Zeigler, Andrew	56
Worrel, Morris	54	Zell, David	19
Worrell, Jonathan	101	Zimmerman, Jacob	90
Wortzheiser, Christian	42	Zinck, Jacob	48
Wright, John	75	Zipolt, John Martin	78

T

www.ingramcontent.com/pod-product-compliance
Lightning Source LLC
Chambersburg PA
CBHW060356080526
44583CB00012B/341